Anointed for Battle

By:

Shane Brown

The Prayer of Faith Ministry

P.O. Box 536

New Caney, Texas 77357

www.prayerfaithministry.com

Anointed for Battle

(Revised and Expanded Edition)

Copyright © 2010, 2011 by Shane Brown

ISBN 978-1-257-71853-5

Unless noted, all Scripture quotations are taken from the King James Version of the Holy Bible

Scripture taken from the New King James version ® Copyright © 1982 by Thomas Nelson, Inc. Used by permission. All rights reserved.

Scripture quotations taken from THE AMPLIFIED BIBLE, Copyright © 1954, 1958, 1962, 1964, 1965, 1987 by The Lockman Foundation. All rights reserved. Used by permission.

Scripture quotations taken from the New American Standard Bible, Copyright © 1960, 1962, 1963, 1968, 1971, 1972, 1973, 1975, 1977, 1995 by The Lockman Foundation. Used by permission.

CONTENTS

The Armor of God
The Weapons of Our Warfare
The Baptism of the Holy Spirit
The Five Signs of a Believer
God is No Respecter of Persons
The Authority of the Believer
Exposing Witchcraft and the Occult
The Power of Your Words
The Pre-Adamic Race
Conditional Security of the Believer
The Curse of the Law
Our Identity in Christ
The Deeper Things of God
The Pre-Tribulation Rapture

We are living in the last days, time is getting short, and now more than ever before, the Church - the body of Christ, needs to have a wake-up call concerning the spiritual war that is before us. There's a battle raging in the heaven-lies, and the body of Christ has been given the spiritual weapons to use to successfully defeat the devil at his every turn. **1 Peter 5:8 says - "Be sober, be vigilant; because your adversary the devil, as a roaring lion, walketh about seeking whom he may devour."** Now really look at what this verse says. It says that the devil is seeking whom he MAY devour, not whom he can devour. If you are walking in your full authority in Christ

and are rooted and grounded in Christ and His Word, the devil cannot devour you - because you know the authority you have, and you resist him. Those who may be devoured by the devil, are those who leave him an open door. It may just be a crack, but
that is all the devil needs to gain entry into your life, and to wage an all out attack against you, and your family, and all that concerns you. Verse 9 of the same chapter goes on to tell us to resist the devil steadfast in our faith. We as believers must be on our toes daily, always alert and watchful. The most successful way to truly resist the devil is by being fully submitted to God and His Word. Let's look at James chapter 4:

***James 4:7* "Submit yourselves therefore to God. Resist the devil, and he will flee from you."**

There's the key to resisting the devil - we stay submitted to God. Many people like to quote the last half of that verse, but fail to realize the cause and effect of the entire verse. First we must submit to God, then we can resist the devil, and then he has no choice but to flee. Submitting to God and His Word involves many things, including knowing what the Word says, and knowing what our spiritual weapons of warfare are. I like to call these weapons Christian Power Tools. God has given us many weapons to use to wage successful war against the devil and his demons. Satan doesn't play fair, and his only goal is to steal, kill, and destroy. (See **John 10:10**). We, on the other hand, can rejoice in the fact that - "**....the Son of God was manifested that he might destroy the works of the devil.**" (1 John 3:8 b).

The Christian Power Tools we have been given are not like natural weapons we see out in the world. If a Christian were to try and use a natural, physical weapon against the devil, they would only be laughed at and ridiculed. The weapons that we have in the spiritual realm are God-given, God-ordained weapons that get the job done, and leave satan and his cohorts screaming for mercy. Let's take a look now at second Corinthians chapter 10:

2 Corinthians 10:3-6 **"For though we walk in the flesh, we do not war after the flesh: (For the weapons of our warfare are not carnal, but mighty through God to the pulling down of strongholds;) Casting down imaginations, and every high thing that exalteth itself against the knowledge of God, and bringing into captivity every thought to the obedience of Christ; And having in a readiness to revenge all disobedience, when your obedience is fulfilled."**

The Word of God says that though we are walking in a fleshly body, we don't do warfare according to the flesh, or worldly standards. Our warfare is done according to the leading of the Holy Spirit, and the weapons that God has given to us. The weapons we have are not natural, but spiritual, and they pull down and demolish strongholds that the devil has erected in the lives of so many. Before we delve into what these weapons of warfare are, let's take a look at the second portion of 2 Corinthians 10. It says that we are to cast down imaginations and every high thing that exalts itself against the knowledge of God. This passage of Scripture is referring to the negative thoughts and suggestions that the devil will implant in your mind. We must remember that the mind is the devil's battlefield. If he can get you to think on his nasty thoughts long enough, eventually he can tempt you to even act on what he says. This is where we again have to be submitted to God, and resist the devil and his thoughts. Any thought, reasoning, philosophy, attitude, or mindset that is contrary to the Word of God is to be cast down, and brought into captivity to the obedience of Christ. If we want to be successful in spiritual warfare, then we need to daily renew our minds in God's Word, and not be led astray by the lying thoughts and suggestions of the devil. Sickness, disease, lack, poverty, oppression, depression, etc, are all high things that exalt themselves against the knowledge of God, and need to be cast down.

***Romans 12:2* "And be not conformed to this world: but be ye transformed by the renewing of your mind, that ye may prove what is that good, and acceptable, and perfect will of God."**

We don't need to conform to this world's system - we need to be transformed by renewing our minds daily in God's holy Word. This is how we can prove what is that good and acceptable, and perfect will of God.

The Bible says to think on the things that are lovely, and honest, and worthy of praise. So in other words, we think on the things of God's kingdom. Let's take a look at the book of Philippians:

Philippians 4:8 **"Finally, brethren, whatsoever things are true, whatsoever things are honest, whatsoever things are just, whatsoever things are pure, whatsoever things are lovely, whatsoever things are of good report; if there be any virtue, and if there be any praise, think on these things."**

When we start thinking on God's thoughts and His attributes, then our thoughts and ways will be in line with His. Whatever we hear, see, read, etc, must line up with the Word of God. The Word of God is the final measure and authority. If it's not in line with the Word, then throw it out. Don't even give it a second thought. Once we recognize that the mind is the battlefield where satan tries to gain entrance, then we are well on our way to wage spiritual warfare against him and his demons. Now let's look at the weapons of warfare that will help us to defeat the attacks of the enemy, and gain victory in our lives. First off, we have to be properly dressed for battle. A Christian soldier caught without wearing their armor is going to be in some serious trouble. We must be dressed for success!

THE ARMOR OF GOD:

Ephesians 6:10-18 **"Finally, my brethren, be strong in the Lord, and in the power of His might. Put on the whole armour of God, that ye may be able to stand against the wiles of the devil. For we wrestle not against flesh and blood, but against principalities, against powers, against the rulers of the darkness of this world, against spiritual** wickedness in high places. Wherefore take unto you the whole armour of God, that ye may be able to withstand in the evil day, and having done all, to stand. Stand therefore, having your loins girt about with truth, and having on the breastplate of righteousness; And your feet shod with the preparation of the Gospel of peace; Above all, taking the shield of faith, wherewith ye shall be able to quench all the fiery darts of the wicked. And take the helmet of salvation, and the sword of the Spirit, which is the Word of God: Praying always with all prayer and supplication in the Spirit, and watching thereunto with all perseverance, and supplication for all saints"

We are admonished to put on the whole armor of God, not just parts of it. We must be fully dressed, and standing our ground. We are not fighting with flesh and blood people.

Our fight is with the devil and all of his demonic kingdom. The first piece of armor we have is *the belt of truth*. When we receive the truth and continue in it, we will be made free. The truth is the very Word of God. Look what Jesus said in the eighth chapter of the book of John:

***John 8:31-32* "If ye continue in my Word then are ye my disciples indeed; And ye shall know the truth, and the truth shall make you free."**

The truth - the Word of God that we know and put into practice will make us free. Knowing the truth about someone else won't make us free. We must know the truth for ourselves, and walk in it all the time.

The second piece of armor we have is *the breastplate of righteousness*. When a person becomes a Christian, they are made the righteousness of God in Christ Jesus. A person who is righteous is in right standing with God. The devil is the enemy of all righteousness, and he hates it, and will do all he can to tear down righteousness, and replace it with unrighteousness. This is why we need to guard our hearts with the breastplate of righteousness. We even see insight into this breastplate of righteousness in the Old Testament. Let's look at Isaiah chapter 59:

Isaiah 59:17 **"For he put on righteousness as a breastplate, and a helmet of salvation upon his head; and he put on the garments of vengeance for clothing, and was clad with zeal as a cloak."**

We can definitely see that the righteousness of God is indeed a powerful weapon against the devil's devices. Isaiah chapter 61 tells us that the Lord clothes us with the garments of salvation and a robe of righteousness. (See **Isaiah 61:10**).

The third piece of armor is *the Gospel boots of peace*. Don't ever be caught barefoot when going to battle against the devil and his kingdom. These Gospel boots that we have been given are not some little wimpy ballet slippers that we prance around in. No, the shoes we have in the spiritual war are steel-toed, Gospel-branded boots that kick the devil right in the teeth. Believers are to be always prepared to present the Gospel of Jesus Christ. Jesus Christ Himself is the Prince of Peace, and peace is what crushes Satan under our feet. Look at this passage from the book of Romans:

Romans 16:20 **"And the God of peace shall bruise Satan under your feet shortly. The grace of our Lord Jesus Christ be with you. Amen."**

Isaiah 9:6 **"For unto us a child is born, unto us a Son is given: and the government shall be upon his**

shoulder: and his name shall be called Wonderful, Counselor, The mighty God, The everlasting Father, The Prince of Peace."

The fourth piece of armor we have is *the shield of faith*. Faith is what a believer lives by. The Bible declares in **Hebrews 10:38 a, "Now the just shall live by faith."** (See also **Habakkuk 2:4, Romans 1:17, Galatians 3:11**). The believer is admonished to fight the good fight of faith in the first book of Timothy. It's a good fight because we win!

1 Timothy 6:12 **"Fight the good fight of faith, lay hold on eternal life, whereunto thou art also called, and hast professed a good profession before many witnesses."**

The devil uses fear and intimidation, but when a child of God lifts up his shield of faith, all the darts of the devil will fall to the ground - being of no effect. Faith brings God on the scene. We had to have faith to believe there is a God, and faith to receive Jesus Christ as our Savior and Lord. The devil hates our faith, so what better way to come against him - with the shield of faith. Faith pleases God, and causes the devil to run in terror. Make no mistake about it. In fact, we see in the book of Hebrews that without faith, we cannot please God. It is only by faith. We are faith people of a faith God.

Hebrews 11:6 **"But without faith it is impossible to please him: for he that cometh to God must believe that he is, and that he is a rewarder of them that diligently seek him."**

All fear is - is false evidence appearing real. The devil is the master deceiver, and if he can get you to believe his lies and tricks, he can lure you into his web of darkness. Don't be deceived. Just lift up that faith shield, and watch the devil's darts and arrows be null and void.

The fifth piece of spiritual armor we have to fight the good fight of faith is *the helmet of salvation.* As with the breastplate of righteousness, the book of Isaiah also mentions the Lord putting on a helmet of salvation. Let's look again at Isaiah 59:

Isaiah 59:17 **"For he put on righteousness as a breastplate, and an helmet of salvation upon his head; and he put on the garments of vengeance for clothing, and was clad with zeal as a cloak."**

The purpose of the helmet of salvation is to guard our minds from the attacks of the enemy. As I said earlier, your mind is the devil's battlefield, his playground. We have to renew our minds daily in the Word of God. It is essential that every believer guard his or her thoughts. The enemy loves to mess with your head, so be alert, and refuse everything that he offers you. Cast down every negative, Word-opposing thought, and let God's saving strength guard your mind. This spiritual war is very real, and we all need to be guarded at all times.

***2 Corinthians 10:5* "Casting down imaginations and every high thing that exalteth itself against the knowledge of God, and bringing into captivity every thought to the obedience of Christ."**

The sixth piece of armor is *the Sword of the Spirit - The Word of God*. This piece of our spiritual armor is one of the most important. The Sword of the Spirit is the very Word of God. Like I always say, we can wield a natural, physical sword and try to poke the enemy with it all day, and it won't do a thing. However, when we wield the Sword of the Spirit, it causes damage in the kingdom of darkness. The way we use this weapon is by speaking forth the Word of God - out loud, out of our very mouths. The devil can't read your thoughts, but he certainly can hear you when you speak. So speak the Word of God, and watch the devil be cut up into bits!

Hebrews 4:12 **"For the Word of God is quick, and powerful, and sharper than any two-edged sword, piercing even to the dividing asunder of soul and spirit, and of the joints and marrow, and is a discerner of the thoughts and intents of the heart."**

The very Word of God gets the job done. The Word is a quick and powerful spiritual weapon that has the ability to tear down strongholds and every other demonic thing the enemy uses against us. The Word of God is sharper than a natural sword, and when the Word comes out of our mouths in faith, all principalities and demon powers have to listen and obey. They have no choice in the matter.

Psalms 149:6 "Let the high praises of God be in their mouth, and a two-edged sword in their hand."

Psalms 68:11 "The Lord gave the word: great was the company of those that published it."

Revelation 19:15 "And out of his mouth goeth a sharp sword, that with it he should smite the nations: and he shall rule them with a rod of iron: and he treadeth the winepress of the fierceness and wrath of Almighty God."

Jeremiah 23:29 "Is not my Word like as a fire? Saith the Lord; and like a hammer that break-eth the rock in pieces?"

The Word has power to turn situations around. The Word is a spiritual fire, a supernatural hammer that breaks the demonic realm into pieces. The Word of God also burns up all the dross and brings deliverance to a situation. All believers need to learn to talk back to the devil like Jesus did. Tell the devil - IT IS WRITTEN. That's using the Word of God against him. (See **Matthew 4:1-11, Luke 4:1-13, Deuteronomy 8:3**). When all else fails, the Word never will. It is eternal, and the absolute truth. Period.

Isaiah 40:8 **"The grass withereth, the flower fadeth: but the Word of our God shall stand for ever."**

Psalms 119:160 **"Thy word is true from the beginning: and every one of thy righteous judgments endureth for ever."**

Although many don't count *prayer* as a part of the armor, we must understand that it's a very important part of a Christian's armor. Don't go into warfare without being covered in prayer. Prayer is powerful, and every

Christian needs to pray daily.

***Ephesians 6:18* "Praying always with all prayer and supplication in the Spirit, and watching thereunto with all perseverance and supplication for all saints."**

This verse primarily focuses on intercession, and being a watchman on the wall, but the main point we need to look at is "in the Spirit." This is referring to praying in our Holy Ghost language - tongues.

***Jude 20* "But ye, beloved, building up yourselves on your most holy faith, praying in the Holy Ghost."**

When we pray in the Spirit, it helps build up our spirits, and makes us a better witness for Christ. Praying in the Spirit helps us also to better hear from God more clearly. Many times when we try praying in the understanding - we arrive at a roadblock, so to speak.

Our flesh wants to get in the way. However, when we pray in the Holy Spirit, He helps us to overcome the flesh, and intercedes on our behalf. The Holy Spirit gives us the words to speak, and they bypass our minds and go straight to the throne room of God the Father. Let's look at a Scripture passage from the book of Romans:

Romans 8:26-27 **" Likewise the Spirit also helpeth our infirmities: for we know not what we should pray for as we ought: but the Spirit itself maketh intercession for us with groanings which cannot be uttered. And he that searcheth the hearts know-eth what is the mind of the Spirit, because he maketh intercession for the saints according to the will of God."**

There's the key right there - "according to the will of God." Many Christians pray just any old thing in their natural languages and think it's

God's will. We have to realize that if it's contrary to the Word, then it shouldn't be spoken. Words have power, both positive and negative, and we better be praying God- inspired prayers. This is why it is so vital that we pray a lot in the Spirit. The devil cannot understand us when we pray in the Spirit, so it angers him even more. Good ! That's what we want. The devil is a liar, and he has no power over a blood bought, Holy Spirit baptized believer who knows who they are in Christ, and knows how to use the weapons God has given them. Fasting is another important part of prayer, and when done the Lord's way, will produce wonderful results. Look at Isaiah 58:

Isaiah 58:6-8 **"Is not this the fast that I have chosen? To loose the bands of wickedness, to undo the heavy burdens, and to let the oppressed go free, and that ye break every yoke? Is it not to deal thy**

bread to the hungry, and that thou bring the poor that are cast out to thy house? When thou seest the naked, that thou cover him; and that thou hide not thyself from thine own flesh? Then shall thy light break forth as the morning, and thine health shall spring forth speedily: and thy righteousness shall go before thee; the glory of the Lord shall be thy re-reward."

After the listing of the Armor of God in Ephesians 6, we see some good advice about the believer using their mouth to speak the Word of God boldly. Listen up church, because this is extremely important, as is everything else we are going to cover in this book.

Ephesians 6:19-20 **"And for me, that utterance may be given unto me, that I may open my mouth boldly, to make known the mystery of the gospel, For which I am an**

ambassador in bonds: that therein I may speak boldly, as I ought to speak."

Just having on the full armor of God isn't enough. We have to also open our mouths and boldly proclaim the Gospel of Christ, and boldly take authority over the devil and his demonic camp of intruders. It's time for Christians to be bold! It's time to start taking back what the devil has stolen from us! And believe me, the devil has stolen a lot!

Proverbs 28:1 **"The wicked flee when no man pursueth: but the righteous are bold as a lion."**

Romans 1:16 **"For I am not ashamed of the gospel of Christ: for it is the power of God unto salvation to every one that believeth; to the Jew first, and also to the Greek."**

Never be ashamed of the Gospel,

always boldly and aggressively proclaim the good News of Jesus Christ - the salvation, healing, deliverance, and abundance that He offers. When you're as bold as a lion, the devil will have to back off and run for his life! There's far too many wimpy, mealy-mouthed Christians. It's time for the true believers to rise up. It's time to stand up and be counted as those who are armed and anointed for battle. God has got our backs, and His strength is upon us, so we are well equipped. God's strength will see us through any situation that arises. So take the limits off of God, and allow Him to move freely in your life. God is our strength, and He will back us up.

Psalms 28:8 **"The Lord is their strength, and he is the saving strength of his anointed."**

Psalms 18:39 **"For thou hast girded me with strength unto the battle: thou hast subdued under me those**

that rose up against me."

Romans 13:12 **"The night is far spent, the day is at hand: let us therefore cast off the works of darkness, and let us put on the armour of light."**

Verse 14 **"But put ye on the Lord Jesus Christ, and make not provision for the flesh to fulfill the lusts thereof."**

We are told to put on the Lord Jesus Christ - and that is what we are doing when we put on the Armor of God. Truth, righteousness, peace, faith, salvation, The Word of God - are all descriptions of Jesus Himself, so when we put on the whole armor of God, we are actually putting on Jesus Christ. He is our supernatural covering, glory be to God! No wonder the devil hates the armor of God. No wonder he tries to blind the eyes of believers. The devil knows that once we get a hold of the truth, he's done for! So, now that we are properly dressed for battle with our spiritual armor in place, we need to fill up our arsenal with the weapons of our warfare that are mighty in pulling down strongholds. There are many weapons, and I want to focus on some of the most powerful ones we have been given.

THE NAME OF JESUS:

There is power in the mighty Name of Jesus. Demons tremble at the very mention of the Name of Jesus. Every knee has to bow at the Name of Jesus. Just think about it this way - every thing has a name. Everything is called something. A chair, a table, a restaurant, a church, a person. The Name of Jesus as above all those names and every name that is named both now, and ever will be. A lot of people like to throw around names so they can feel important or recognized. They like for people to know they are in good with someone who is well known or such. They like to name drop. Well, when we speak the Name of Jesus - His Name gets more attention than any name we can come up with. The devil's kingdom shudders in terror when the Name of Jesus is spoken in faith. The Name of Jesus defeats the darkness, and brings deliverance to those held captive by satan. Look what the Word says in Philippians chapter 2:

Philippians 2:9-11 **"Wherefore God also hath highly exalted him, and given him a name which is above every name. That at the name of Jesus every knee should bow of things in heaven, and things in earth, and things under the earth; And that every tongue should confess that Jesus Christ is Lord, to the glory of God the Father."**

Every knee has to bow at the mighty Name of Jesus. This includes sickness, disease, lack, oppression, depression. All of it has to bow to the Name of Jesus Christ. If you happen to be in a crisis situation, just call upon the Name of the Lord Jesus. Speak His Name out loud, and He will watch over you and protect you from all harm. The Bible says that the Name of the Lord is a strong Tower that we can run to at all times. You can always count on the Name of Jesus!

***Proverbs 18:10** **"The name of the Lord is a strong tower: the righteous runneth into it, and is safe."**

Learn to be a name dropper today. Learn the power and authority in the Name of Jesus. Christians have been given the power of Attorney to use the Name of Jesus. As Christ's representatives, we have the right and the privilege of using His Name to defeat all manner of darkness and deception. At the Name of Jesus every knee must bow, and every tongue must confess! Praise God for that awesome Name!

Psalms 9:9-10 **"The Lord also will be a refuge for the oppressed, a refuge in times of trouble. And they that know thy name will put their trust in thee: for thou, Lord, hast not forsaken them that seek thee."**

In the Name of Jesus there is salvation, healing, deliverance, and true wholeness and peace. Nothing missing, nothing broken, nothing ever ignored. It says there in Psalms 9 that they that KNOW His Name. That's one of the keys right there. We must know the Name of Jesus, and we must know that there is anointed power in that Name! Let's look now at the book of **Acts**:

Acts 3: 6-7 **"Then Peter said, Silver and gold have I none; but such as I have give I thee: In the name of Jesus Christ of Nazareth rise up and**

walk. And he took him by the right hand, and lifted him up: and immediately his feet and ankle bones received strength."

Acts 3:16 "And his name through faith in his name hath made this man strong, whom ye see and know: yea, the faith which is by him hath given him this perfect soundness in the presence of you all."

Acts 4:12 "Neither is there salvation in any other: for there is none other name under heaven given among men, whereby we must be saved."

In the Name of Jesus, the man at the Gate Beautiful was healed. Peter told him that he didn't have silver or gold, but he did have the Name of Jesus. As he spoke that Name, immediately the lame man received strength in his feet and ankle bones. Healing comes through the Name of Jesus! That's a powerful weapon to throw a death blow at the devil!

David, who lived under the Old Covenant also knew the power in the Name of the Lord. When he went to battle against the giant Goliath, he went armed with the Name of Almighty God, and He came out victoriously!

1 Samuel 17:45 **"Then said David to the Philistine, Thou comest to me with a sword, and with a spear, and with a shield: but I come to thee in the name of the Lord of hosts, the God of the armies of Israel, whom thou hast defied."**

1 Samuel 17:50-51 **"So David prevailed over the Philistine with a sling and with a stone, and smote the Philistine, and slew him; but there was no sword in the hand of David. Therefore David ran, and stood upon the Philistine, and took his sword, and drew it out of the sheath**

thereof, and slew him, and cut off his head therewith. And when the Philistines saw their champion was dead, they fled."

David prevailed over the giant because he went in the Name of the Lord. That was what caused him to be successful over his enemy. David was armed and anointed for battle. What a mighty weapon we have in the Name of Jesus! Don't go to battle without His mighty Name on your lips. Don't let the devil run rough-shod over you. Take your rightful authority over him, and wield your weapons over him. Speak forth that mighty Name of Jesus in faith, and watch the devil and his demons run for the hills! Believe me, they know the power in that Name. And so should each and every one of us too!

THE BLOOD:

Next, we are going to look at the blood. The blood of Jesus is another powerful spiritual weapon in the believer's arsenal. Just the mention of the blood makes the demons tremble and squirm in their seats. The precious shed blood of Jesus has redeeming power, and when a believer receives Jesus as their Savior, they are now blood-bought - they have accepted the sacrifice that Jesus paid for on the Cross at Calvary. The Word says that by the stripes of Jesus we were and are healed. That ought to make you shout and leap for joy!

***Isaiah 53:5* "But he was wounded for our transgressions, he was bruised for our iniquities: the chastisement of our peace was upon him; and with his stripes we are healed."**

***1 Peter 2:24* "Who his own self bare our sins in his own body on the tree, that we, being dead to sins, should live unto righteousness: by whose stripes ye were healed."**

There's healing in the blood of Jesus. There's deliverance in the blood of Jesus. With every stripe that wounded the Lord, we were healed and made whole. We have been bought with the precious blood of Jesus Christ, and have a blood bought right to use the blood as a weapon against all the forces of darkness. The devil and his demons know very well that the blood defeated them at the Cross of Calvary. With every lash on the Lord's back, we were set free and healed, and a death blow was given to the devil. It's no surprise that the devil and his cohorts hate even the mention of the blood. They know the power in the blood, and so should you if you want to be free from the enemy's aggressive onslaughts. I highly recommend that every believer daily plead the blood of Jesus over their families, their cars, their homes, and over yourself. Apply the blood as a spiritual covering over your life - like a bandage is in the natural. When the blood is applied and spoken in faith, no demon can trespass where the blood is covering. Be aggressive, and tell the enemy, satan - the blood of Jesus is against you ! Trust me, he will flee ! The blood of Jesus is what cleanses us from sin and washes us from iniquities. We should never just casually talk about the blood. The blood is our very life source, and is what redeems us, glory be to God. Look at these Scriptures:

Ephesians 1:7 **"In whom we have redemption through his blood, the forgiveness of sins, according to the riches of his grace."**

Leviticus 17:11 **"For the life of the flesh is in the blood: and I have given it to you upon the altar to make an atonement for your souls: for it is the blood that maketh an atonement for the soul."**

When we plead, or apply the blood, we

are decreeing and declaring God's divine protection over us and all that concerns us, and we are forbidding the devil's agenda in our lives. When a believer pleads the blood of Jesus, they are literally closing the door in the devil's face. The Word is very clear how a believer overcomes the devil. It is by the blood of the Lamb, and the word of our testimony.

Revelation 12:11 **"And they overcame him by the blood of the Lamb, and by the word of their testimony, and they loved not their lives unto the death."**

If you are a true believer, then you should have a testimony, and your testimony should include how the blood has made you victorious and more than a conqueror. The blood and your testimony is a double dose of ammunition against the devil and his host of wickedness in the wicked heavenlies. Just to be clear, Jesus did not spill His blood, He shed His blood for us - on purpose, it was no accident - it was the very will of God the Father. The blood of Jesus speaks, and it still speaks today. It is warm and alive.

Hebrews 12:23-24 **"To the general assembly and church of the firstborn, which are written in heaven, and to God the Judge of all, and to the spirits of just men made perfect, And to Jesus the mediator of a new covenant, and to the blood of sprinkling, that speaketh better things than that of Abel."**

The blood of Abel represents death, but the blood of Jesus represents life, and that more abundantly. (See **John 10:10, 1 Peter 1:18-19**). Thank God we are in a new covenant based upon better promises. We don't have the blood of bulls and goats, we have the precious blood of Jesus that is alive and powerful, and redemptive.

Hebrews 9:12-14 "**Neither by the blood of goats and calves, but by his own blood he entered in once into the holy place, having obtained eternal redemption for us. For if the blood of bulls and of goats, and the ashes of an heifer sprinkling the unclean, sanctifieth to the purifying of the flesh: How much more shall the blood of Christ, who through the eternal Spirit offered himself without spot to God, purge your conscience from dead works to serve the living God?"**

The people of the Old Testament did not have the kind of Covenant we have as New Testament believers. Yet, even under the Old covenant, the book of Exodus tells us that when Israel put blood on the door facings, the destroyer could not come in. (See **Exodus 12:21-23**). Back then they used animal blood which serves as a type and shadow of the blood of Jesus which we have now, and which ratifies us much better protection under our new Covenant which is established upon much better promises. A physical weapon is operated with our hands, but a spiritual weapon is operated with our mouths in faith. This is how we apply the blood of Jesus - by saying it in absolute faith. When we do, the destroyer - the devil, must flee at once! There is wonder working power in the blood of Christ Jesus, and when spoken out of our mouths in faith, it has the power to quench all the fiery darts of the evil one. Just let the blood of Jesus speak for you and your household!

PRAISE:

The next spiritual weapon in the believer's arsenal we are going to look at is praise. Yes, praise is a spiritual weapon for the anointed believer. Praise puts the devil to flight because he hates praises to God because he wants all the praise. The devil fell because of pride. He wanted to be exalted and praised above God. (See **Isaiah 14:12-23, Ezekiel 28:11-19**). It's no wonder that he is defeated when praises are lifted up to Almighty God. The Word tells us that God inhabits the praises of His people. He is enthroned upon praises lifted up unto Him. (See **Psalms 22:3**). We were created to praise. It's what we were made to do as sons and daughters of the Most High. We are King's kids, and as such, we are to be praisers! Let's look at a couple of Scriptures from the book of Psalms that really brings this to light:

Psalms 102:18 **"This shall be written for the generation to come: and the people which shall be created shall praise the Lord."**

Psalms 43:21 **"This people have I formed for myself; they shall shew forth my praise."**

When you praise God, you magnify Him and His kingdom. Praise includes warfare. The devil has an aggressive agenda, and will not stop his deceitful strategies. However, we as blood-bought, Spirit-filled believers with our weapons of warfare can come into his camp and plunder his house. Praise is one of the weapons that will help us to successfully keep the devil under our feet where he belongs. As believers, we must praise our way to victory. One of the best places in Scripture about the power of praise and overcoming the enemy is found in 2 Chronicles chapter 20. That warfare of praise that I just mentioned is clearly evident in this passage of Scripture. Let's take a look:

2 Chronicles 20:13-30 **"And all Judah stood before the Lord, with their little ones, their wives, and their children. Then upon Jahaziel the son of Zechariah, the son of Benaiah, the son of Jeiel, the son of**

Mattaniah, a Levite of the sons of Asaph, came the Spirit of the Lord in the midst of the congregation; And he said, Hearken ye, all Judah, and ye inhabitants of Jerusalem, and thou King Jehoshaphat, Thus saith the Lord unto you, Be not afraid nor dismayed by reason of this great multitude; for the battle is not yours, but God's. To morrow go ye down against them: behold, they come up by the cliff Ziz; and ye shall find them at the end of the brook, before the wilderness of Jeruel. Ye shall not need to fight in this battle; set yourselves, Stand still, and see the salvation of the Lord with you, O Judah and Jerusalem: fear not, nor be dismayed; to morrow go out against them: for the Lord will be with you. And Jehoshaphat bowed his head with his face to the ground: and all Judah and the inhabitants of Jerusalem fell before the Lord, worshipping the Lord. And the Levites, of the children of the

Kohathites, and of the children of the Korhites, stood up to praise the Lord God of Israel with a loud voice on high. And they rose early in the morning, and went forth into the wilderness of Tekoa: and as they went forth, Jehoshaphat stood and said, Hear me, O Judah, and ye inhabitants of Jerusalem; Believe in the Lord your God, so shall ye be established; believe his prophets, so shall ye prosper. And when he had consulted with the people, he appointed singers unto the Lord, and that should praise the beauty of holiness, as they went out before the army and to say, Praise the Lord; for his mercy endureth for ever. And when they began to sing and to praise, the Lord set ambushments against the children of Ammon, Moab, and Mount Seir, which were come against Judah; and they were smitten. For the children of Ammon and Moab stood up against the inhabitants of Mount Seir, utterly to slay and destroy them: and when they hade made an end of the inhabitants of Seir, every one helped to destroy another. And when Judah came toward the watch tower in the wilderness, they looked unto the multitude, and behold, They were dead bodies fallen to the earth, and none escaped. And when Jehoshaphat and his people came to take away the spoil of them, they found among them in abundance both riches with the dead bodies, and precious jewels, which they stripped off for themselves, more than they could carry away: and they were three days in the gathering of the spoil, it was so much. And on the fourth day they assembled themselves in the valley of Berachah; for there they blessed the Lord: therefore the name of the same place was called, the Valley of Berachah, unto this day. Then they returned every man of Judah and Jerusalem, and Jehoshaphat in the

**forefront of them, to go again to Jerusalem with joy: for the Lord had made them to rejoice over their enemies. And they came to Jerusalem with psalteries and harps and trumpets unto the house of the Lord. And the fear of God was on all the kingdoms of those countries, when they had heard that the Lord fought against the enemies of Israel. So the realm of Jehoshaphat was quiet:
for his God gave him rest round about."**

When they began to give God praise, God came upon the scene, and set ambushments against their enemies. He also restored so much back to them, that it took three days to gather all of it. Praise brings an overflow of God's blessings into your life! When we begin to give God praise, He will inhabit that praise, and He will come upon the scene, and will set an ambushment against our enemy - the devil. God will restore everything that the devil has stolen, and will supply us with an overflow of all that we need. And our God will lift up a standard against the enemy and his onslaught.

Isaiah 59:19 **"So shall they fear the name of the Lord from the west, and his glory from the rising of the sun. When the enemy shall come in like a flood, the Spirit of the Lord shall lift up a standard against him."**

Psalms 149:5-9 **"Let the saints be joyful in glory: let them sing aloud upon their beds. Let the high praises of God be in their mouth, and a two-edged sword in their hand; To execute vengeance upon the heathen, and punishments upon the people; To bind their kings with chains, and their nobles with fetters of iron; To execute upon them the judgment written: this honor have all his saints. Praise ye the Lord."**

Even in the midst of a storm, determine to be a person of praise, and you will see God move on your behalf, and interrupt the devil's plan. There's delivering power in praise, and it's up to each of us as believers to open our mouths, and speak forth praise unto God. When we do, God will be there in our midst, and He will deliver us from all the evil plans of the devil, and those whom he uses. Just begin to praise God, no matter what things look like, and you will see your situation and surroundings change. The devil wants you to look at the situation from his angle - don't do it. Look to God because He is your Source, and He will cause you to come out victoriously.

Psalms 150:6 **"Let every thing that hath breath praise the Lord. Praise ye the Lord."**

THE PRAYER OF AGREEMENT:

The next weapon of warfare we are going to look at is The Prayer of Agreement. Did you know that there is power in agreement? When believers of like precious faith come together and agree in prayer, God promises that it shall be done, and that He would be right there in the very midst of us. Let's look at the book of Matthew:

Matthew 18:19-20 **"Again I say unto you, That if two of you shall agree on earth as touching anything that they shall ask, it shall be done for them of my Father which is in heaven. For where two or three are gathered together in my name, there am I in the midst of them."**

The word "touching" in this passage means to surround and to grasp. So we can say that whatever we surround and grasp hold of by faith - will be done by Father God in heaven. The word "agreement" means harmony. It means to harmonize together, and to be a symphony. This symphony of agreement and unity involves the Godhead - Father, Son, Holy Spirit, as well as believers. The Godhead operates in symphony - working together as One. Let's look at first John chapter 5:

1 John 5:4-8 **"For whatsoever is born of God overcometh the world: and this is the victory that overcometh the world, even our faith. Who is he that overcometh the world, but he that believeth that Jesus is the Son of God? This is he that came by water and blood, even Jesus Christ; not by water only, but by water and blood. And it is the Spirit that beareth witness, because the Spirit is truth. For there are three that bear record in heaven, the Father, the Word, and the Holy Ghost: and these three are one. And there are three that bear witness in**

earth, the Spirit, and the water, and the blood: and these three agree in one."

The Godhead, which is the Trinity, always works together as a symphony. They are One, and never work apart from each other. We too are to be as one. One body in total symphony. What a weapon against the devil! Now let's take a look at verses 14 and 15 of the same chapter to see the results of the symphony:

1 John 5:14-15 **"And this is the confidence that we have in him, that, if we ask any thing according to his will, he heareth us: And if we know that he hear us, whatsoever we ask, we know that we have the petitions that we desired of him."**

God's Word is His will - so when we ask in prayer about something from His Word that He has promised us, it's a done deal. Those who are not a part of God's symphony of agreement won't get the results they desire.

The prayer of agreement is not to be done with just anyone. We really need to understand that. Not everyone who says they are a believer really are one. We have to make sure we are coming into agreement with those who are on the same page as we are. Both parties must be in total agreement with what is being prayed for. This is essential if we want to receive the right results and flow with God's symphony.

Amos 3:3 **"Can two walk together, except they be agreed?"**

1 Corinthians 1:10 **"Now I beseech you, brethren, by the name of our Lord Jesus Christ, that ye all speak the same thing, and that there be no divisions among you, but that ye be perfectly joined together in the same mind and in the same judgment."**

Just think about it. If you're praying for the manifestation of your healing, would you want to pray with someone who doesn't believe in divine healing? I don't think so! We must come into agreement with those who believe in the full counsel of God's Word, which definitely includes divine healing for all. The prayer of agreement is a powerful spiritual weapon because when the anointed army of God comes together in agreement, the devil and his demons are out numbered. The anointed prayers of the saints do great damage to the kingdom of darkness, and brings God's perfect will to fruition on earth. Look what the Word says in Matthew chapter 6:

Matthew 6:10 **"Thy kingdom come. Thy will be done in earth, as it is in heaven."**

How is it in heaven? Well, in heaven there's no sickness, no lack, no oppression, no depression. Start praying God-centered prayers, and you will see God's will on earth as it is in heaven. When we do this, the devil's plan is thwarted. The anointing, which is the power and presence of the Holy Spirit, is present when believers come together in unity - in total agreement. Let's look at the book of Psalms - chapter 133. This really brings this point to light:

Psalms 133:1-3 **" Behold, how good and how pleasant it is for brethren to dwell together in unity ! It is like the precious ointment upon the head, that ran down upon the beard, even Aaron's beard: that went down to the skirts of his garments; As the dew of Hermon, and as the dew that descended upon the mountains of Zion: for there the Lord commanded the blessing, even life for evermore."**

Ointment is another symbol or type of the anointing. Here in this passage of

Scripture we see that the anointing goes from the top of our heads right down to our feet. The power of the Holy Spirit of God covers us, and puts us in the place of His commanded blessings. We see another description of the power of unity in the book of Acts.

Acts 1:4-5, 8 **"And being assembled together with them, commanded them that they should not depart from Jerusalem, but wait for the promise of the Father, which saith he, ye have heard of me. For John truly baptized with water, but ye shall be baptized with the Holy Ghost not many days hence."**

Verse 8 **"But ye shall receive power, after that the Holy Ghost is come upon you: and ye shall be witnesses unto me both in Jerusalem, and in all Judaea, and in Samaria, and unto the uttermost part of the earth."**

Acts 2:1-4 "And when the day of Pentecost was fully come, they were all with one accord in one place. And suddenly there came a sound from heaven as of a rushing mighty wind, and it filled all the house where they were sitting. And there appeared unto them cloven tongues like as of fire, and it sat upon each of them. And they were all filled with the Holy Ghost, and began to speak with other tongues, as the Spirit gave them utterance."

In chapter one of Acts, we see Jesus telling those that were assembled together to wait for the promise of the Holy Spirit. In chapter two we see the fulfillment of this promise, and those who were gathered together were all in one accord, in one place. They were in unity - in perfect agreement, and they received the promised Holy Spirit. The power of agreement and unity among believers is essential. First off, we must be in agreement with the Lord

Jesus, and then come into agreement with those who also are in agreement with Jesus. Believers must choose their prayer partners very wisely. Don't just pick anyone. Be very discerning, and make sure that they are on the same page as you are - in agreement with God and His Word, which is His will.

BINDING AND LOOSING:

The next area of the believer's weapons of warfare that I want to look at is binding and loosing. This particular area of spiritual warfare goes along with the prayer of agreement that we just studied. Let's start by reading in the book of Matthew - chapter 16:

Matthew 16:13-19 **"When Jesus came into the coasts of Caesarea Philippi, he asked his disciples, saying, Whom do men say that I the Son of man am? And they said, some say that thou are John the Baptist:**

some, Elias, and others Jeremias, or one of the prophets. He saith unto them, But whom say ye that I am? And Simon Peter answered and said, Thou art the Christ, the Son of the living God. And Jesus answered and said unto him, Blessed art thou, Simon Barjona: for flesh and blood hath not revealed it unto thee, but my Father which is in heaven. And I say also unto thee, That thou art Peter, and upon this rock I will build my church; and the gates of hell shall not prevail against it. And I will give unto thee the keys of the kingdom of heaven: and whatsoever thou shalt bind on earth shall be bound in heaven; and whatsoever thou shalt loose on earth shall be loosed in heaven."**

Jesus asked His disciples who the people thought He was. They told Him that some thought He was John the Baptist, some thought He was Elijah, and some even said He was Jeremiah.

Jesus questioned them further and asked them - but Who do you say that I am? Peter answered and told Him, You are the Christ, the Son of the living God. Peter received revelation knowledge from God the Father. He didn't get this information from a fleshly, carnal source. Just to be clear on this, Jesus wasn't calling Peter the rock. Obviously, the Church could never be built upon a man. The rock that Jesus was referring to in this statement is the revelation that Jesus was and is the Christ - meaning the Anointed One in His anointing. This revelation is the very basis of the Church. Jesus said that the gates of hell shall not prevail against the Church - meaning the true Church, the body of Christ that walks in the power and anointing of the Holy Spirit. The Holy Spirit Himself anoints us - the believer, and with that anointed power on us, and in us, we have the authority to chase the devil and his ugly demon henchmen away. They cannot prevail against the anointed Church ! Jesus went on the say that He has given us the keys of the kingdom of heaven. Notice, He didn't say we had the keys TO the kingdom. He said we have the keys OF the kingdom. There's a difference. Think about it. When you have the keys to someone's house, or the keys to a hotel, you may have a key. But you have limited access. However, when you have the keys OF someone's house or the keys OF a hotel, it means you have access to everything ! When Jesus said He has given us the keys of the kingdom, He was saying we have access to everything in His kingdom. No limits whatsoever. All the good things that God has, and that's all He has is good things, belongs to us. Keys represent authority, and power, and ownership. We have all the keys needed to enter the kingdom and overcome all of the powers of darkness. Whatever we bind on earth, is bound in heaven, This means that whenever a believer takes authority, God will back us up.

Matthew 12:29 **"Or else how can one enter into a strongman's house, and spoil his goods, except he first bind the strong man?, and then he will spoil his house."**

A strongman is a demonic spirit sent by the devil to afflict, harass, and destroy all those who will accept it. As Christians, we have authority over these foul spirits, in the Name of Jesus. We have the keys of the kingdom that will plunder the works of the devil. When we bind, we are tying up, and forbidding the devil and his foul spirits access into our lives. When we loose, we are allowing the blessings of God and the anointing of the Holy Spirit to work in the situation. We have the keys that will loose blessings of God that the devil wants to steal from us. We see more on binding and loosing again in the book of Matthew, in chapter 18:

Matthew 18:18-20 "Verily I say unto you, Whatsoever ye shall bind on earth shall be bound in heaven: and whatsoever ye shall loose on earth shall be loosed in heaven. Again I say unto you, That if two of you shall agree on earth as touching any thing that they shall ask, it shall be done for them of my Father which is in heaven. For where two or three are gathered together in my name, there am I in the midst of them."

Again, we must agree with God, and come together with those who also agree with God, and when we do, Jesus said He would be right there in the midst of us. The prayer of agreement and the prayers of binding and loosing bring the Lord right on the scene to work on our behalf. Don't be deceived, the devil is an equal opportunity destroyer, and he will attempt to destroy anyone who is not grounded in the Word of God. With the keys of the kingdom we can open the doors of God's awesome blessings for our lives. With these supernatural keys, we can dominate, and take back what the devil has stolen. Believe me, the devil has stolen a lot, but when a believer knows their authority and position in Christ, we can recover all that was stolen from us. If we want to be the glorious Church that is victorious and fit for God's Kingdom, then we better know how to use the keys that God has given us. There are many strongholds and barriers in people's lives that need to be cast down, and when we know what God's Word says, and act upon it, we will see many set free from the devil's clutches.

***James 1:22* "But be ye doers of the Word, and not hearers only, deceiving your own selves."**

Self deception is a killer, and Satan will use it against any who fail to be doers of God's Word. That is why it is extremely important that we do what God's Word says to do. Just listening to it won't cut it. We must be doers of the Word. When we are, we will see all the blessings and the benefits of Christ and His awesome Kingdom!

THE WORD OF GOD:

In order to be successful over the attacks of the devil, we must know the Word. We saw earlier what a mighty spiritual weapon the Word of God is - our Sword of the Spirit. It's all about the Word. That's a major part of being anointed for battle - we are Word minded people, not world minded. That's one of the big problems with a lot of the church today. They are so world-minded, that they don't even give heed to what The Word says. We must not be one of those. We must stand firm upon The Word of God, and never be shaken. The Word is forever, and is what brings light to every dark situation. Let's look at a few passages from the book of Psalms that clearly bring this point home:

Psalms 119:89 "For ever, O Lord, thy Word is settled in heaven."

Psalms 119:105 "Thy Word is a lamp unto my feet, and a light unto my path."

Psalms 119:130 "The entrance of thy words giveth light; it giveth understanding unto the simple."

Psalms 138:2 "I will worship toward thy holy temple, and praise thy name for thy loving kindness and for thy truth: for thou hast magnified thy Word above all thy name."

God even magnifies His Word above all His Name. The Word of God is powerful, and we need to be built up in the Word, and when we are, the devil better watch out because the anointed army of God is going to plunder his camp. Never fear though, because God has our backs. His Word does not return void. God's Word stands forever, and prospers in what He sends it to do. The very Word of God is alive, and active, and will make the devil's plan of no effect.

Hebrews 4:12 **"For the Word of God is quick, and powerful, and sharper than any two-edged sword, piercing even to the dividing asunder of soul and spirit, and of the joints and marrow, and is a discerner of the thoughts and intents of the heart."**

Isaiah 55:11 **"So shall my Word be that goeth forth out of my mouth: it shall not return unto me void, but it shall accomplish that which I please, and it shall prosper in the thing whereto I sent it."**

Psalms 140:7 **"O God the Lord, the strength of my salvation, thou hast**

covered my head in the day of battle."

God is our everlasting strength, and He has us covered with His divine protection. No foe can withstand this mighty covering. They may try to attack, but to no avail. Our God has us covered. We have divine insurance!

Psalms 91:1-4 **"He that dwelleth in the secret place of the most High shall abide under the shadow of the Almighty. I will say of the Lord, He is my refuge and my fortress: my God; in Him will I trust. Surely he shall deliver thee from the snare of the fowler and from the noisome pestilence. He shall cover thee with his feathers, and under his wings shalt thou trust: his truth shall be thy shield and buckler."**

The key to being given divine protection is dwelling and abiding in God's secret place - in His presence.

When we know Who God is and place our total trust in Him, nothing can shake us or move us. We are steadfast in the Lord, and no man, woman, child, or devil will tell us any different. We have to have that kind of tenacity if we want to truly succeed in this spiritual battle. We can't afford to give up, or be complacent. We have to take the bull by the horns, and determine - I mean aggressively determine to stand upon God's Word, never looking any other way.

Psalms 125:1 **"They that trust in the Lord shall be as mount Zion, which cannot be removed, but abideth for ever."**

God's truth - His Word, is our shield and buckler. We have no fear because God is on our side, and we live by total faith in Him. We don't have to fear man one iota.

Psalms 3:3, 6-7 **"But thou, O Lord,**

art a shield for me; my glory, and the lifter up of mine head."

Verses 6-7 "I will not be afraid of ten thousands of people, that have set themselves against me round about. Arise, O Lord; save me, O my God: for thou hast smitten all mine enemies upon the cheek bone; thou hast broken the teeth of the ungodly."

Hebrews 13:6 "So that we may boldly say, The Lord is my Helper, and I will not fear what man shall do unto me."

We don't have to be afraid at all, because God didn't give us a spirit of fear. Fear comes from the devil, not from God. Don't give in to the lies of religion. And yes, religion is a spirit - a foul one at that. You heard me right. Jesus didn't give us a religion, He gave us a relationship. And He gave us a sound mind. It's right in the Word:

2 Timothy 1:7 **"For God hath not given us the spirit of fear; but of power, and of love, and of a sound mind."**

Don't put up with the devil's fear, learn to recognize it for what it is - a foul spirit, and then bind it, and cast it out. Loose the power of love and a sound mind - the mind of Christ, to fill you to the full. Now let's continue in Psalms 91:

Psalms 91:9-12 **"Because thou hast made the Lord, which is my refuge, even the most High, thy habitation; There shall no evil befall thee, neither shall any plague come nigh thy dwelling. For he shall give his angels charge over thee, to keep thee in all thy ways. They shall bear thee up in their hands, lest thou dash thy foot against a stone."**

When we make God our habitation -

our permanent dwelling place, we are promised to be protected from all evil. Not one plague or destruction will harm us, for God gives His angels charge over us to keep us in all of our ways. We see another Psalm that gives us further insight into the ministry of God's angels. Psalms 34:

Psalms 34:7 **"The angel of the Lord encampeth round about them that fear him, and delivereth them."**

God Almighty is our Deliverer, and He releases His angels to watch over us. God safeguards all those who trust in Him, and who habitually abide in Him. There is a two-fold condition to this - we must abide in Him, and also let His Word abide in us. When we truly do these two things, Jesus said that whatever you desire would be yours. This is cause and effect in action. This is how the Kingdom works.

John 15:7 **"If ye abide in Me, and my words abide in you, ye shall ask what ye will, and it shall be done unto you."**

The things we will ask for will be God's desires because when we are truly abiding in Him, the only things we will want are those things of Him and His Kingdom. What we thought were our desires, will fade away into the background. As we abide in God's manifest presence, His desires will become our desires. Remember, though - we must commit ourselves completely unto Him. God must be number one in our lives. Let's continue on in Psalms 91:

Psalms 91:14-16 **"Because he hath set his love upon me, therefore will I deliver him: I will set him on high, because he hath known my name. He shall call upon me, and I will answer him: I will be with him in trouble; I will deliver him, and**

honor him. With long life will I satisfy him, and shew him my salvation."

In the spiritual battle there is a lot of opposition around us. However, we can rejoice and stand our ground because we know Who our God is, and we set our love and attention on Him, and He promises to answer us when we call on Him, and to deliver us from trouble. In the Secret Place, we have been given long life. Life that no demon or devil can touch. The key to not being touched by the devil is abiding fully in Christ Jesus and His Word - and He is the Word. This is clearly outlined in the first chapter of the book of John:

John 1:1, 14 **"In the beginning was the Word, and the Word was with God, and the Word was God."**

Verse 14 **"And the Word was made flesh, and dwelt among us, (and we**

beheld his glory, the glory as of the only begotten of the Father), full of grace and truth."

This brings me to the next thing I want to discuss and teach you. To be anointed for battle, we need to understand what the anointing of the Holy Spirit really is.

THE BAPTISM OF THE HOLY SPIRIT:

Isaiah 10:27 **"And it shall come to pass in that day, that his burden shall be taken away from off thy shoulder, and his yoke from off thy neck, and the yoke shall be destroyed because of the anointing."**

The anointing of the Holy Spirit of God destroys the yoke of bondage, and removes every burden off of every shoulder. That is the presence of God at work. Christ is not Jesus' last name. Christ means The Anointed One in His anointing. This is referring to the power of the Holy Spirit Who came upon Jesus and anointed Him for His earthly ministry. Jesus did no miracles until He was anointed with the Holy Spirit. That is when His ministry of miracles and healing, and deliverance began. Look at these two Scriptures:

Matthew 3:16 **"And Jesus, when he was baptized, went up straightway out of the water: and lo, the heavens were opened unto him, and he saw the Spirit of God descending like a dove, and lighting upon him: And lo a voice from heaven, saying, This is my beloved Son, in whom I am well pleased."**

Acts 10:38 **"How God anointed Jesus of Nazareth with the Holy Ghost and with power: Who went about doing good, and healing all that were oppressed by the devil; for God was with him."**

God the Father anointed Jesus with the Holy Spirit, and with power. Like I said, this is when His miracle ministry began - when He became the Christ, the Anointed One in His anointing. Just think about this, a lot of people will acknowledge that Jesus was a good man, and that He walked this earth. However, when you ask them about the power of the Holy Spirit, and the Gifts of the Spirit, oh people get defensive. Many will say that these Gifts and ministries of the Holy Spirit are not valid for today. What a lie of the devil ! All of God's Gifts are for today. See, this is what the anti-Christ spirit is against - it's against the power of the Holy Spirit. Jesus became the Christ and started His ministry of healing and deliverance, and we too as the body of Christ are to imitate Christ. We must recognize the antichrist spirit, and take authority over it in Jesus Name. Look at the Scriptures:

1 John 2:18-22 **"Little children, it is**

the last time: and as ye have heard that anti-Christ shall come, even now are there many antichrist's; whereby we know that it is the last time. They went out from us, but they were not of us; for if they had been of us, they would no doubt have continued with us: but they went out, that they might be made manifest that they were not all of us. But ye have an unction from the Holy One, and ye know all things. I have not written unto you because ye know not the truth, but because ye know it, and that no lie is of the truth. Who is a liar but he that denieth that Jesus is the Christ? He is anti-Christ that denieth the Father and the Son."

We must use discernment and God's wisdom, and not just believe every spirit just because they say the Name of Jesus. There are a lot of people who mouth the Name of Jesus, but not in faith. Those are just mockers and unbelievers. We must test the spirits. This is essential because there are countless deceivers out there just waiting to come in and wreck havoc on the church. One of their number one goals is to discredit the power of the Holy Spirit. So it is essential that we know what God's Word says, and we don't just take everything as gospel. Test the spirits!

1 John 4:1-6 **"Beloved, believe not every spirit, but try the spirits whether they are of God: because many false prophets are gone out into the world. Hereby know ye the Spirit of God: Every spirit that confesseth that Jesus Christ is come in the flesh is of God: And every spirit that confesseth not that Jesus Christ is come in the flesh is not of God: and this is that spirit of anti-Christ, whereof ye have heard that it should come; and even now already is it in the world. Ye are of God, little children, and have overcome**

them: because greater is He that is in you, than he that is in the world. They are of the world: therefore speak they of the world, and the world heareth them. We are of God: he that know-eth God heareth us; he that is not of God heareth not us. Hereby know-eth we the Spirit of truth, and the spirit of error."

Don't believe every individual or church, or ministry that says they are from God. The Bible makes it very clear that there are many false prophets out there. The true test, the true measure is confessing that Jesus Christ has come in the flesh. Of course Jesus Christ came and walked this earth as a flesh and blood man. This is truth, and we know it. But just think about it - almost everyone is willing to admit that part, even cults and all other manner of unbelievers. The true measure, the litmus test - is confessing that Jesus Christ has come to live and dwell in the flesh of the believer through the Baptism of the Holy Spirit. Many, if not all, of those same people who will say Jesus walked the earth as a flesh and blood man, won't tell you He comes to actually live in your flesh and in my flesh. Why? Well, it's because they are antichrist. Remember, Christ means the Anointed One, The Messiah, in His anointing. The antichrist spirit is against the power of the Holy Spirit. It's against tongues, healing, and deliverance. The reason God's Word says to try or test the spirits, is because many will believe lies and not check things out for themselves. The devil is a master deceiver and he doesn't want people to know the truth about the work of the Holy Spirit. Let's now look at second John verses seven through eleven for further insight into this:

2 John 7-11 **"For many deceivers are entered into the world, who confess not that Jesus Christ is come in the flesh. This is a deceiver and an anti-**

Christ. Look to yourselves, that we lose not those things which we have wrought, but that we receive a full reward. Whosoever transgresseth, and abideth not in the doctrine of Christ, hath not God. He that abideth in the doctrine of Christ, he hath both the Father and the Son. If there come any unto you, and bring not this doctrine, receive him not into your house, neither bid him God speed: For he that biddeth him God speed is partaker of his evil deeds."

The Word of God says that anyone who comes to you and doesn't bring the doctrine of Christ - the Anointed One in His anointing, then we are not to receive them into our home, and we are not even to give them a greeting. If you give them a greeting all you're doing is encouraging their false doctrine, and partaking of their errors. If someone won't tell you that Jesus Christ has come to live in your flesh by the Holy Spirit, then the Word says they are not of God, they are deceivers. They must bring the full doctrine of Christ Jesus, including all of His teaching. Healing, deliverance, and prosperity, Who Christ is, and what He taught. That is what we are to embrace. Anything other than that is to be refused. The antichrist spirit is a vicious spirit that seeks to diminish the work of the Holy Spirit. If someone even limits the work of the Holy Spirit and His Gifts, then they have an anti-Christ spirit. Again, we must test all things according to the Word of God. That's the final, absolute authority.

1 Thessalonians 5:19-22 **"Quench not the Spirit. Despise not prophesying. Prove all things; hold fast that which is good. Abstain from all appearance of evil."**

The Word tells us to abstain from even the appearance of evil. So if something even remotely appears evil, then we are not to touch it. We are to abhor it, and only partake of what is good. The antichrist spirit is evil, and it only seeks to deceive and to discredit the work of the Holy Spirit. Don't be deceived. Let God show you what is truth, and what is not. Remember, God and His Word are One and the same.

Romans 12:9 b **"….Abhor that which is evil; cleave to that which is good."**

We as Christians are to cleave to the Spirit of Truth, which is the Holy Spirit of God. Receiving the Holy Spirit is different from receiving Jesus as Savior. When a person receives Jesus as their Savior, they become blood bought. That means they are saved.

Romans 10:9-10 **"That if thou shalt confess with thy mouth the Lord Jesus, and shalt believe in thine heart that God hath raised him from**

the dead, thou shalt be saved. For with the heart man believeth unto righteousness; and with the mouth confession is made unto salvation."

Verse 13 **"For whosoever shall call upon the name of the Lord shall be saved."**

This is referring to initial salvation. The Baptism of the Holy Spirit is a separate experience from initial salvation, and it is the Holy Spirit Who adopts us into the body of Christ. Just receiving Jesus as Savior is being saved FROM condemnation, but receiving the Holy Spirit baptism is being saved TO the glory. This glory is referring to the glorification of our bodies when our bodies will be made like Jesus. The glorification and Rapture of the Church are fast approaching us. This is no time to be sitting on our hands. We must walk in the anointed power of God. Look at these Scriptures:

Ephesians 1:13-14 "In whom ye also trusted, after that ye heard the word of truth, the gospel of your salvation: in whom also after that ye believed, ye were sealed with that Holy Spirit of promise, Which is the earnest of our inheritance until the redemption of the purchased possession, unto the praise of his glory."

Colossians 1:26-27 "Even the mystery which hath been hid from ages and from generations, but now is made manifest to his saints: To whom God would make known what is the riches of the glory of this mystery among the Gentiles; which is Christ in you, the hope of glory"

The Holy Spirit draws us to Jesus, then we in turn are to receive the Holy Spirit. The evidence that we have the

Holy Spirit is speaking in tongues - our prayer language. Let's look to the Word to see the Scriptural foundation, starting with the book of Matthew:

Matthew 3:11 **"I indeed baptize you with water unto repentance: but he that cometh after me is mightier than I, whose shoes I am not worthy to bear: he shall baptize you with the Holy Ghost, and with fire."**

This is talking about John the Baptist baptizing people in water unto repentance in the Name of Jesus. He goes on to tell us that it is the Lord Jesus Who will baptize us with the Holy Spirit and with fire. We also see another Scriptural witness that the Baptism of the Holy Spirit is a separate experience from initial salvation, in the Gospel of John, seventh chapter:

John 7:37-39 **"In the last day, that great day of the feast, Jesus stood**

and cried, saying, If any man thirst, let him come unto me, and drink. He that believeth on me, as the Scripture hath said, out of his belly shall flow rivers of living water. (But this spake he of the Spirit, which they that believe on him should receive: for the Holy Ghost was not yet given; because that Jesus was not yet glorified)."

We see also in the Gospel of John that Jesus makes it very clear that we are to be born again of the Holy Spirit. This wasn't a suggestion or "if you want to" thing. This is essential. Look at chapter 3:

John 3:3-7 **"Jesus answered and said unto him, Verily, verily, I say unto thee, Except a man be born again, he cannot see the kingdom of God. Nicodemus saith unto him, how can a man be born when he is old? Can he enter the second time into his mother's womb, and be born? Jesus**

answered, verily, verily, I say unto thee, except a man be born of water and of the Spirit, he cannot enter into the kingdom of God. That which is born of the flesh is flesh; and that which is born of the Spirit is spirit. Marvel not that I said unto thee, ye must be born again."

We must be born of both our natural birth water, and of the Holy Spirit, which is the baptism of the Holy Spirit and the evidence of tongues. Jesus clearly says that believers shall be baptized with the Holy Ghost, and that power would be upon them. Let's look at the book of Acts as we continue our study on the baptism of the Holy Spirit:

Acts 1:5, 8 **"For John truly baptized with water; but ye shall be baptized with the Holy Ghost not many days hence."**

Verse 8 **"But ye shall receive power,**

after that the Holy Ghost is come upon you: and ye shall be witnesses unto me both in Jerusalem, and in all Judea, and in Samaria, and unto the uttermost part of the earth."

Acts 2:1-4 "And when the day of Pentecost was fully come, they were all with one accord in one place. And suddenly, there came a sound from heaven as of a rushing mighty wind, and it filled all the house where they were sitting. And there appeared unto them cloven tongues like as of fire, and it sat upon each of them. And they were all filled with the Holy Ghost, and began to speak with other tongues, as the Spirit gave them utterance."

In chapter one of Acts they were waiting on the promise of the Holy Spirit, and in chapter two we see the fulfillment of this promise from the Lord. On the day of Pentecost, believers in the Lord Jesus received the Baptism of the Holy Spirit, and became born again Christians, adopted into the body of Christ.

Galatians 3:27 **"For as many of you as have been baptized into Christ have put on Christ."**

Romans 8:15-16 **"For ye have not received the spirit of bondage again to fear; but ye have received the Spirit of Adoption, whereby we cry, Abba, Father. The Spirit itself beareth witness with our spirit, that we are the children of God."**

The Spirit of Adoption - the Holy Spirit of God is Who adopts us into the family of God - the true body of Christ. This is how we become a son of God, and can call God our Daddy.

Romans 8:14 **"For as many as are led by the Spirit of God, they are the sons of God."**

The key here is we need to listen to the Holy Spirit, and follow His leadings. He is our Teacher, and He will always guide us into all truth, for He is the Spirit of Truth. Let's continue on now to see more Scriptural evidence of the baptism of the Holy Spirit, and the evidence of tongues, starting with Acts chapter 16:

***Acts 19:1-6* "And it came to pass, that while Apollos was at Corinth, Paul having passed through the upper coasts came to Ephesus: and finding certain disciples, He said unto them, Have ye received the Holy Ghost since ye believed? And they said unto him, We have not so much as heard whether there be any Holy Ghost. And he said unto them, Unto what then were ye baptized? And they said, unto John's baptism. Then said Paul, John verily baptized with the baptism of repentance, saying unto the people, that they should believe on Him which should**

come after him, that is, on Christ Jesus. When they heard this, they were baptized in the name of the Lord Jesus. And when Paul lad laid his hands upon them, the Holy Ghost came on them; and they spoke with tongues, and prophesied."

These believers at Ephesus hadn't even heard about the Holy Spirit, much less received Him. These disciples at Ephesus received Jesus as Savior. They were blood bought, but not Spirit filled. Well all that changed. We see that after Paul talked with them, they received the Holy Spirit and became born again Christians. We know this because they spoke with tongues - which is the evidence of the Holy Spirit baptism. It's no wonder that the devil hates the work of the Holy Spirit. It's also no wonder that the antichrist spirit is so prevalent in these last days. The enemy's agenda is fierce, but the true Church, the anointed body of Christ, has the power on the inside of us to thwart the devil's plans. I encourage you if you have not already, receive the baptism of the Holy Spirit, and watch your life be transformed, and He will also empower you to be an even greater witness than ever before. The next thing that I want us to take a look at is the five signs of the believer, and the authority of the believer. These two truths, just like all that we have studied, are essential if we want to be truly anointed for battle. Successful spiritual warfare happens when we as believers know who we are in Christ, know the authority we have in Christ, and we walk in that authority.

THE FIVE SIGNS OF A BELIEVER:

Mark 16:15-20 **"And he said unto them, Go ye into all the world, and preach the Gospel to every creature. He that believeth shall be saved; but he that believeth not shall be damned. And these signs shall follow them that believe; In my name shall**

they cast out devils; they shall speak with new tongues; They shall take up serpents; and if they drink any deadly thing, it shall not hurt them; they shall lay hands on the sick, and they shall recover. So then after the Lord had spoken unto them, he was received up into heaven, and sat on the right hand of God. And they went forth, and preached every where, the Lord working with them, and confirming the Word with signs following. Amen."

In the Great Commission that Jesus gave to His disciples, which also includes us, He listed five signs that would follow those who believe. Jesus said that those who believe and are baptized shall be saved. As we established earlier, believing on Jesus - receiving Him as Savior, means you are blood bought. The baptism referred to in this passage refers to the baptism of the Holy Spirit, not water baptism. Water baptism is Scriptural and is a wonderful thing, but it is not a salvation requirement. It is an outward showing of an inward work. The reason we know that this baptism is Holy Spirit baptism, is because the signs that follow are all the work of the Holy Spirit. Now if you don't believe anything, Jesus said you will be condemned. Being blood bought is the first step, then receiving the baptism of the Holy Spirit to be fully born again, and a member of the body of Christ. The five signs of the believer are: casting out devils, speaking in new tongues, being unharmed by anything deadly, taking up serpents, and laying hands on the sick who shall recover. If someone tells you that they are a believer, ask them if they believe these five signs. Ask them if they walk in these signs. You will find that there are a lot of unbelieving believers out there. Jesus didn't say these signs would follow this certain denomination, or this group, or that group, no, He said these signs shall follow them that believe. So if you are truly a believer, then these signs should be following you. This is not just for a select few, this is for all those who believe in Christ. Sadly, most churches and ministries are so caught up in brownie bake-offs, Tupperware parties, and fund-raisers, that they don't even realize that they have gotten off into unbelief. Far too many Churches have become country clubs and entertainment facilities - "seeker friendly churches". Where's the Gospel? Where's the power and anointing of the Holy Spirit? Where's healing and deliverance? The church has fallen asleep in the enemy's lap. They're trying to appease people instead of pleasing God. There's no power in their lives or ministries because they have ignored Jesus' great commission. So we are going to start right now, and examine these five signs of the believer.

CASTING OUT DEMONS:

Matthew 10:1, 7-8 "And when he had called unto him his twelve disciples, he gave them power against unclean spirits, to cast them out, and to heal all manner of sickness and all manner of disease."

Verses 7-8 "And as ye go, preach, saying, the kingdom of heaven is at hand. Heal the sick, cleanse the lepers, raise the dead, cast out devils: freely ye have received, freely give."

Mark 3:14-15 "And he ordained twelve, that they should be with him, and that he might send them forth to preach, and to have power to heal sickness, and to cast out devils."

Mark 6:7, 12-13 "And he called unto him the twelve, and began to send them forth by two and two; and gave them power over unclean spirits"

Verses 12-13 "And they went out, and preached that men should repent. And they cast out many devils, and anointed with oil many that were sick, and healed them."

Luke 9:1-2 "Then he called his twelve disciples together, and gave them power and authority over all devils, and to cure diseases."

Luke 10:17-20 "And the seventy returned again with joy, saying, Lord, even the devils are subject unto us through thy name. And he said unto them, I beheld Satan as lightning fall from heaven. Behold, I give unto you power to tread on serpents and scorpions, and over all the power of the enemy: and nothing shall by any means hurt you. Notwithstanding in this rejoice not, that the spirits are subject unto you; but rather rejoice, because your names are written in heaven."

Jesus cast out demons, His disciples cast out demons, and we - His body on this earth are to cast out demons. Jesus has delegated His authority to us, and we have the anointing of the Holy Spirit in us when we are baptized in the Spirit. This is being anointed for battle. Spiritual battle against all the forces of darkness. We haven't a thing to fear, because Jesus said nothing shall by any means hurt us. The anointing and the blood is our protective covering. We have the power, and authority to invade the enemy's camp and bind and cast out every demon there is. Demons have to bow at the very Name of Jesus Christ of Nazareth! Now let me tell you, a born-again Christian cannot be POSSESSED, but they can be OPPRESSED by demons, and demons can most certainly attach to the flesh, where they can afflict just as much harm. However, we do not have to put up with demon harassment of any kind, whether from believers or unbelievers. We have the anointing in and upon us to cast those evil spirits out and off. In fact, as we have seen, Jesus said that this is one of the signs that follow those who believe. He said plainly in **Mark 16:17** that we are to cast out demons (devils). In the book of Acts we see the Apostle Paul taking authority of a demon spirit of divination. Let's take a look:

Acts 16:16-18 **"And it came to pass as we went to prayer, a certain damsel possessed with a spirit of divination met us, which brought her masters much gain by soothsaying: The same followed Paul and us, and cried, saying, These men are the servants of the most high God, which shew unto us the way of salvation. And this did she many days. But Paul, being grieved, turned and said to the spirit, I command thee in the name of Jesus Christ to come out of her. And he cam out the same hour."**

Now notice that Paul spoke to the spirit, and not to the girl. Remember that our fight is not with flesh and blood, but with demonic principalities and powers, and wicked forces of darkness. (See **Ephesians 6:12**). Demonic activity is very real, and Jesus has given us - the church, the body of Christ, the commission to go forth and cast out demons. It makes no difference what form they are in, we are to cast them out. Let's now move on to the next sign of a believer.

SPEAKING WITH NEW TONGUES:

As we saw earlier, speaking in tongues is the initial evidence that a person is baptized with the Holy Spirit.

Acts 2:4 **"And they were all filled with the Holy Ghost, and began to speak with other tongues, as the Spirit gave them utterance."**

Acts 19:6 "And when Paul had laid his hands upon them, the Holy Ghost came on them; and they spake with tongues, and prophesied."

1 Corinthians 12:10 b "….to another divers kinds of tongues; to another the interpretation of tongues."

1 Corinthians 14:2, 22, 39 "For he that speaketh in an unknown tongue speaketh not unto men, but unto God: for no man understand him; howbeit in the Spirit he speaketh mysteries."

Verse 22 "Wherefore tongues are for a sign, not to them that believe, but to them that believe not: but prophesying serveth not for them that believeth not, but for them which believe."

Verse 39 "Wherefore, brethren, covet to prophesy, and forbid not to speak with tongues."

As I noted earlier, praying in the Spirit helps us to better hear from God, and builds up our faith. Praying in the Spirit also helps us to be a better witness. Look at this verse from the book of Jude:

***Jude 20* "But ye, beloved, building up yourselves on your most holy faith, praying in the Holy Ghost."**

(Also see **Romans 8:26-27** again for further study on this).

Praying in the Spirit is the only perfect prayer, because it is the Holy Spirit Himself praying through us unto the Father. We are doing the speaking, but it is the Holy Spirit Who gives us the words to speak forth. If you haven't received the Baptism of the Holy Spirit, I would highly suggest that you do right now. Don't be deceived by the false teachers out there who will try and tell you that tongues have ceased.

That is not true at all. Tongues are for today just as much as they were for the early church. One of the Scriptures that gets misquoted often is from first Corinthians chapter 13. Let's examine this verse:

1 Corinthians 13:8 **"Charity never faileth: but whether there be prophecies, they shall fail; whether there be tongues, they shall cease; whether there be knowledge, it shall vanish away."**

Now notice what this Scripture says. It says that tongues shall cease, not that they have ceased. It's so clear in the Word, yet so many so called believers want to twist it and make it say something that it doesn't. The second portion of this verse says that knowledge shall vanish away too, but has it yet? No it hasn't. We need to understand what is being said here in this verse. It's referring to the future, not now. Tongues have NOT ceased, and knowledge has NOT vanished away. Jesus said that those who believe on Him shall speak with new tongues. (See **Mark 16:17**). Now let's move on to the next sign that follows the believer.

TAKING UP SERPENTS:

When Jesus said that believers shall take up serpents, He wasn't talking about dancing around with snakes, trying to look spiritual. Taking up serpents refers to dealing with the demonic, and removing the venomous poison of false doctrines. Any doctrine that goes against the Word of God and doesn't line up with the Word, is a false doctrine, and we are to expose it, and remove it from our lives. Satan is the serpent, so when we take up serpents, we are taking up satan, and casting him, and his doctrines of demons out.

1 Timothy 4:1-2 **"Now the Spirit**

speaketh expressly, that in the latter times some shall depart from the faith, giving heed to seducing spirits, and doctrines of devils; Speaking lies in hypocrisy; having their conscience seared with a hot iron."

2 Timothy 4:2-4 **"Preach the Word; be instant in season, out of season; reprove, rebuke, exhort with all longsuffering and doctrine. For the time will come when they will not endure sound doctrine; but after their own lusts shall they heap to themselves teachers, having itching ears; And they shall turn away their ears from the truth, and shall be turned unto fables."**

In the last days, which we are in, many will depart from faith in Christ, and will heap up for themselves teachers that tickle their ears and tell them what they want to hear. The Word of God calls this a doctrine of demons. We are to preach and teach the whole Word, without compromise, and without worrying what people will say or think. False teachings will abound more and more as we get closer to the end. We must not be deceived, we must know the Word of God, and evict false teachings from our lives and from our churches.

2 Peter 2:1-2 **"But there were false prophets also among the people, even as there shall be false teachers among you, who privily shall bring in damnable heresies, even denying the Lord that bought them, and bring upon themselves swift destruction. And many shall follow their pernicious ways; by reason of whom the way of truth shall be evil spoken of."**

Matthew 24:24 **"For there shall arise false Christs, and false prophets, and shall shew great signs and wonders; insomuch that, if it were possible, they shall deceive the very** elect."

We must know the Truth, and stand upon it. Those who don't know the Truth, and just let everything in, will be lured into the devil's trap. False doctrine is poison, and it eats like a cancer, like gangrene. The venomous poison of false doctrine will stunt the growth of the believer, and make them an easy target for the devil's onslaught.

2 Timothy 2:15-18 **"Study to shew thyself approved unto God, a workman that needeth not to be ashamed, rightly dividing the Word of truth. But shun profane and vain babblings: for they will increase unto more ungodliness. And their word will eat as doth a canker; of whom is Hymenaeus and Philetus; who concerning the truth have erred, saying that the resurrection is past already; and overthrow the faith of some."**

We must study to show ourselves approved unto God - and correctly share and teach the Word of God. It is essential that we know the Truth, and that we continue in it. This is how we show ourselves to be Christ's true disciples. True sons of God. We must know the difference between the truth and a lie. God's Word is truth, and anything that is contrary to the Word of God is a lie, and is therefore a venomous serpent that needs to be taken up, and throw out of the church. When we rightly divide the Word, then we can avoid getting into the ugly pit of false doctrine. In the above Scripture from second Timothy, we see the mention of two men who were bringing false doctrines into the church - Hymenaeus and Philetus. It also says that the words that they speak eat like a canker - meaning a cancer, or a poison like gangrene. If you just look all around you, you will see this happening today. That is why we must be rooted and grounded in the Word of

God. When we are, we won't be seduced by the devil's lies and of those whom he uses to utter his venomous poison. Let's now read a couple of passages from the book of Psalms:

Psalms 140:1-3 **"Deliver me, O Lord, from the evil man: preserve me from the violent man; Which imagine mischiefs in their heart; continually are they gathered together for war. They have sharpened their tongues like a serpent; adders' poison is under their lips. Selah."**

Psalms 58:1-5 **"Do ye indeed speak righteousness, O congregation? Do ye judge uprightly, O ye sons of men? Yea, in heart ye work wickedness; ye weigh the violence of your hands in the earth. The wicked are estranged from the womb: they go astray as soon as they be born, speaking lies. Their poison is like the poison of a serpent: they are like the deaf adder that stoppeth her ear;**

Which will not hearken to the voice of charmers, charming never so wisely."

When we expose the venomous poison of false doctrine, it will aid in helping others to get free from it as well. It's the very truth that we know and put into practice that will make us free. Look at John chapter 8:

John 8:31-32 **"If ye continue in my Word, then are ye my disciples indeed; And ye shall know the truth, and the truth shall make you free."**

John 8:36 **"If the Son therefore shall make you free, ye shall be free indeed."**

Any doctrine that denies the Virgin birth and the deity of Christ is a false doctrine. Any doctrine that denies the Trinity is a false doctrine. Doctrines that say that God uses sickness for His glory or to teach you something - this is a false doctrine, a lie from the pit of hell. Doctrines that deny tongues and the Gifts of the Spirit, and any other work of the Holy Spirit, is false doctrine. As we saw earlier, this is the spirit of antichrist at work - the spirit of error. All the cults and false religions out there are also to be avoided. Mormonism, Jehovah Witnesses, Buddhism, Islam, Hinduism, Koran, Christian Science, Roman Catholicism, Calvinism, etc, are all to be avoided. There is only One Way to heaven, and that is through Jesus Christ.

***John 14:6* "Jesus saith unto him, I am the way, the truth, and the life: no man cometh unto the Father, but by me."**

There is one God, externally existent in Three Persons. God the Father, God the Son, God the Holy Spirit. Anyone who does not agree with this is operating under the influence of the enemy - the devil. That may be blunt, but it's the truth. And as we have just seen, it's the truth that shall make you free indeed!

1 John 5:7-8 **"For there are three that bear record in heaven, the Father, the Word, and the Holy Ghost: and these three are one. And there are three that bear witness in earth, the Spirit, and the water, and the blood: and these three agree in one."**

Another false doctrine that believers need to evict from their thinking is the false doctrine that says we are to be broke and downtrodden in order to be truly Christian. What a lie from the devil. The Word of God tells us different. Look at these Scriptures:

3 John 2 **"Beloved, I wish above all things that thou mayest prosper and be in health, even as your soul prospereth."**

2 Corinthians 8:9 "For ye know the grace of our Lord Jesus Christ, that though He was rich, yet for your sakes he became poor, that ye through his poverty might be rich."

Philippians 4:19 "But my God shall supply all your need according to his riches in glory by Christ Jesus."

Psalms 34:9-10 "O fear the Lord, ye his saints: for there is no want to them that fear him. The young lions do lack, and suffer hunger: but they that seek the Lord shall not want any good thing."

Psalms 35:27 "Let them shout for joy, and be glad, that favour my righteous cause: yea, let them say continually, Let the Lord be magnified, which hath pleasure in the prosperity of his servant."

Psalm 23:1 "The Lord is my

shepherd; I shall not want."

Psalms 84:11 "For the Lord God is a sun and shield: the Lord will give grace and glory: no good thing will he withhold from them that walk uprightly."

The devil is the one who steals, kills, and destroys, but Jesus said that He came to give us life more abundantly - and that includes health, wholeness, peace, joy, financial provision, and much more. (See **John 10:10**). Make no mistake about it - Jesus was a rich Man, and He took poverty on the Cross so we could have a life of abundance. Poverty is a curse, and Christ took it and nailed it to the Cross. We are established in God's righteousness. Poverty, lack, oppression, depression, false doctrines, diseases, and sicknesses are all contrary to God's Word. We have the authority to take up these serpents and kick them back to the pit where they belong.

Isaiah 54:14 **"In righteousness shalt thou be established: thou shalt be far from oppression; for thou shalt not fear: and from terror; for it shall not come near thee."**

It is true that Jesus went to the Cross to save us from hell, but salvation is not limited to just that. Salvation means so much more. The Greek word for salvation is "sozo", and it literally means wholeness, soundness, deliverance, safety, preservation, pardon, restoration, and healing. Now let's move on to the next sign that follows the believer.

BEING UNHARMED BY ANYTHING DEADLY:

This is referring to God's divine protection over us, and the anointing of the Holy Spirit upon us. This is why we pray over our food when we eat.

God's protection - the anointing removes anything harmful that might have come into contact with our food or sodas. I always pray over my meals according to **1 Timothy 4:5 - "For it is sanctified by the Word of God and prayer."** When you have God on your side, no disease shall come nigh your dwelling, or in your stomach either !

Psalms 91:9-10 **"Because thou hast made the Lord, which is my refuge, even the Most High, thy habitation; There shall no evil befall thee, neither shall any plague come nigh thy dwelling."**

The anointing will remove anything deadly. We don't have to fear. Neither should we be seduced by doctrines of demons that teach vegetarianism. (See **1 Timothy 4:1-5**). We need to eat both meat and vegetables. God created these to be received with thanksgiving. Like I said, we pray over all our food, and it is sanctified by God's Word and by prayer. Those who dwell in God's presence, and put their trust in Him, have divine protection upon them. The devil may try to attack, but he will fail because God is watching over us. God sends His angels to keep us in all of our ways. (See **Psalms 91:11**). Those of us who are in right standing with God also have these promises from the book of Isaiah to stand upon:

Isaiah 54:14 **"In righteousness shalt thou be established: thou shalt be far from oppression; for thou shalt not fear: and from the terror; for it shall not come near thee."**

Isaiah 54:17 **"No weapon that is formed against thee shall prosper; and every tongue that shall rise against thee in judgment thou shalt condemn. This is the heritage of the servants of the Lord, and their righteousness is of me, saith the Lord."**

No weapon that the devil forms against you will prosper against us as we are walking with the Lord God and proclaiming His truth. We have been established in His righteousness, so all oppression, disease, or plagues have to be far from us. The weapon may be formed, but it will not prosper. It will be made null and void. Jesus told us in the book of Luke that nothing shall hurt us. The key is that we must be walking with Him, doing His will. We must be walking in our authority as believers.

Luke 10:19 **"Behold, I give unto you power to tread on serpents and scorpions, and over all the power of the enemy: and nothing shall by any means hurt you."**

In the book of Acts, we see where Paul the Apostle cam into contact with a literal viper. This beautifully illustrates the divine protection that God gives to all those who trust Him. Let's take a look:

Acts 28:1-6 "And when they were escaped, then they knew that the island was called Melita. And the barbarous people shewed us no little kindness: for they kindled a fire, and received us every one, because of the present rain, and because of the cold. And when Paul had gathered a bundle of sticks, and laid them on the fire, there came a viper out of the heat, and fastened on his hand. And when the barbarians saw the venomous beast hang on his hand, they said among themselves, No doubt this man is a murderer, whom, though he hath escaped the sea, yet vengeance suffer-eth not to live. And he shook off the beast into the fire, and felt no harm. Howbeit they looked when he should have swollen, or fallen down dead suddenly: but after they had looked a great while, and saw no harm come to him, they changed their

minds, and said that he was a god."

It does not matter what we come in contact with, because we have a Covenant relationship with God. God watches over His children faithfully. No deadly thing shall hurt us, because we believe and trust fully in God.

Let's now take a look at two examples from the book of Daniel to further establish that God's people are protected from deadly situations. In chapter 3 we see that there was a decree that was made that whenever the sound of several instruments and all kinds of music was made, that everyone was supposed to fall down and worship a golden image that king Nebuchadnezzar had set up. Now those who did not obey this particular decree were to be cast alive into a burning fiery furnace. The Chaldeans came and told Nebuchadnezzar that their were three men who have failed to honor the decree that was made.

These men were named Shadrach, Meshach, and Abednego. So after hearing this, Nebuchadnezzar gave these men another chance. However, these men were faithful unto God, and still refused to bow down and worship a false god. This made Nebuchadnezzar mad, so he had the furnace heated seven times hotter than usual, and had these three men thrown into the burning flames of fire. (See **Daniel 3:1-22**). Now let's take a look at what happened after God's faithful men were cast into the burning fire:

Daniel 3:23-25 **"And these three men, Shadrach, Meshach, and Abednego, fell down bound into the midst of the burning fiery furnace. Then Nebuchadnezzar the king was astonied, and rose up in haste, and spake, and said unto his counsellors, Did not we cast three men bound into the midst of the fire? They answered and said unto the king, True, O king. He answered and said,**

Lo, I see four men loose, walking in the midst of the fire, and they have no hurt; and the form of the fourth is like the Son of God."

Daniel 3:27-28 "And the princes, governors, and captains, and the king's counsellors, being gathered together, saw these men, upon whose bodies the fire had no power, nor was an hair of their head singed, neither were their coats changed, nor the smell of fire had passed on them. Then Nebuchadnezzar spake, and said, Blessed be the God of Shadrach, Meshach, and Abednego, who hath sent his angel, and delivered his servants that trusted in him, and have changed the king's word, and yielded their bodies, that they might not serve nor worship any god, except their own God."

God protected His faithful men who believed and trusted Him. Even when they were thrown into a burning fiery hot furnace, they came out unharmed by the deadly flames, and they didn't even smell like smoke! He will do the same for us. It's up to us to trust Him, and serve Him with all of our heart. We serve a mighty God, Amen!

Isaiah 43:2 **"When thou passest through the waters, I will be with thee; and through the rivers, they shall not overflow thee: when thou walkest through the fire, thou shalt not be burned; neither shall the flame kindle upon thee."**

Daniel was another man who trusted completely in God, and was unharmed by something deadly. We see in the sixth chapter of the book of Daniel, the king Darius setting Daniel over the whole realm of the kingdom. All of the presidents and the princes were extremely jealous of the favor that Daniel received, so they plotted to destroy him by establishing a petition that stated that if anyone prays or petitions any God or man for thirty days, that that person was to be cast into a den of lions. Now Daniel knew full well the decree was signed and put into action, but it didn't change him nor his relationship with God. Daniel continued to worship and pray to God like he always did. The jealous presidents and princes found Daniel during his prayer time, and blew the whistle on him. So now the king had to throw Daniel into the den of ferocious lions. (See **Daniel 6:1-18**). Now let's take a look at what happened after the king returned the very next morning:

Daniel 6:19-23 **"Then the king arose very early in the morning, and went in haste unto the den of lions. And when he came to the den, he cried with a lamentable voice unto Daniel: and the king spake and said to Daniel, O Daniel, servant of the living God, is thy God, whom thou servest continually, able to deliver thee from the lions? Then said**

Daniel unto the king, O king, live for ever. My God hath sent His angel, and hath shut the lions' mouths, that they have not hurt me: forasmuch as before him innocence was found in me; and also before thee, O king, have I done no hurt. Then was the king exceedingly glad for him, and commanded that they should take Daniel up out of the den. So Daniel was taken up out of the den, and no matter of hurt was found upon him, because he believed in his God."

Daniel, just like Shadrach, Meshach, & Abednego, believed and trusted in God, and was unharmed by the deadly den of ferocious lions. How awesome to know that our God is a God of deliverance and protection!

Daniel 6:27 "He deliver-eth and rescueth, and he worketh signs and wonders in heaven and in earth, who hath delivered Daniel from the power of the lions."

Psalms 145:20 **"The Lord preserveth all them that love him: but all the wicked will he destroy."**

Now let's move on and take a look at the next sign that follows the believer.

LAYING HANDS ON THE SICK - WHO RECOVER:

Jesus said that all those who believe in Him, will lay hands on sick people, and that they would recover. (See **Mark 16:18**). In the Name of Jesus, and the power of the Holy Spirit, we have the authority to lay our hands on those who are sick and bound, and see the healing power of the Lord set them free. That's God's divine healing. Always remember that God is the Healer. We are His conduits, and His healing power flows through our flesh as we lay our hands on those who are bound and tormented. Healing is for today, and the church needs to understand this, and not be swayed by those who oppose healing. The same Jesus Who healed then, still heals today, glory be to God! Let's start by looking at the book of James to lay our Scriptural foundation for divine healing:

James 5:13-16 **"Is any among you afflicted? Let him pray. Is any merry? Let him sing psalms. Is any sick among you? Let him call for the elders of the Church; and let them pray over him, anointing him with oil in the name of the Lord: And the prayer of faith shall save the sick, and the Lord shall raise him up; and if he hath committed sins, they shall be forgiven him. Confess your faults one to another, and pray one for another, that ye may be healed. The effectual fervent prayer of a righteous man availeth much."**

When we lay hands on those who are sick and afflicted, it's the prayer prayed in faith that will save and heal the sick. When we anoint a person with oil, the oil is just a symbol, or a point of contact. There's nothing magical about the olive oil. It's the prayer prayed in faith that saves the sick. Like I said, healing is for today, and is always the will of God. Jesus already healed us 2,000 years ago on the Cross of Calvary. Our part is to obey Him, and let Him use us as an instrument to help others get free. Healing is for God's glory, and belongs to us. The devil can't still it unless you give it to him. Choose today to believe what God said about healing. Don't listen to the false teachers, listen to God. Like I always say, the Word is the final authority.

***Isaiah 53:5* "But he was wounded for our transgressions, he was bruised for our iniquities: the chastisement of our peace was upon him; and with his stripes we are healed."**

Healing is forever settled in heaven. The fact is, God wants you well, and He wants you to help others to get well also. Sickness and disease, and pain are trespassers on the temple of the Holy Spirit. Jesus said by His stripes we were healed. Look at first Peter 2:

1 Peter 2:24 "Who his own self bare our sins in his own body on the tree, that we, being dead to sins, should live unto righteousness: By whose stripes ye were healed."

We were healed on the Cross 2,000 years ago, and we are still healed, glory be to God. Healing is a part of the finished work of the Cross. So lying symptoms have no right on the body of a Christian. We have the authority to lay hands on the sick, and ourselves, and command pain and sickness to go back to the pit, in Jesus Name. We have the keys of the kingdom, and we can bind that spirit of infirmity, and loose the Gifts of healing to flow into our bodies. Jesus healed the sick, and He said those who would believe on Him would do likewise. All throughout the Bible we see countless times where Jesus healed the sick, and where He commissioned His followers to do the same. It's in the Book, and we need to understand it, and apply it to our own lives.

Matthew 8:14-17 **"And when Jesus was come into Peter's house, he saw his wife's mother laid, and sick of a fever. And he touched her hand and the fever left her: and she arose, and ministered unto them. When the even was come, they brought unto him many that were possessed with devils: and he cast out the spirits with his word, and healed all that were sick: That it might be fulfilled which was spoken by Esaias the prophet, saying, Himself took our infirmities, and bare our sicknesses."**

Jesus took our infirmities, and He bore our sicknesses so we would not have to. He did all that for us, so why would someone want to put up with it? Why would a Christian allow the devil to afflict them with pain and tragedy? We have the blood of Jesus, and we have the authority to cancel every attack of the devil, and that most definitely includes sickness and disease. Look at these Scripture passages:

Matthew 10:1, 7-8 **"And when he had called unto him his twelve disciples, he gave them power against unclean spirits to cast them out, and to heal all manner of sickness and all manner of disease."**

Verses 7-8 **"And as ye go, preach, saying, the kingdom of heaven is at hand. Heal the sick, cleanse the lepers, raise the dead, cast out devils: freely ye have received, freely give."**

Matthew 9:35 "And Jesus went about all the cities and villages, teaching in their synagogues, and preaching the gospel of the kingdom, and healing every sickness and every disease among the people."

Matthew 15:29-31 "And Jesus departed from thence, and came nigh unto the sea of Galilee; and went up into a mountain, and sat down there. And great multitudes came unto him, having with them those that were lame, blind, dumb, maimed, and many others, and cast them down at Jesus feet; and he healed them: Insomuch that the multitude wondered, when they saw the dumb to speak, the maimed to be whole, the lame to walk, and the blind to see: and they glorified the God of Israel."

Psalms 103:1-5 "Bless the Lord, O my soul: and all that is within me,

bless his holy name. Bless the Lord, O my soul, and forget not all his benefits: Who forgiveth all thine iniquities; Who healeth all thy diseases. Who redeemeth thy life from destruction; Who crowneth thee with loving-kindness and tender mercies; Who satisfieth thy mouth with good things; so that thy youth is renewed like the eagles."

I could probably write another book just about healing, for the Word of God is filled with Scriptures that clearly show that healing is God's will. These signs shall follow them that believe - they shall lay hands on the sick, and they shall recover. (See **Mark 16:18**). Jesus healed the sick, the disciples healed the sick, and we today as Jesus' disciples - His sons and daughters, are to heal the sick in the Name of Jesus Christ. This, like all of the other signs are not just a suggestion to the church. This a commission - a command from Jesus Himself. The same anointed Holy Spirit that raised Jesus from the dead is here today to help us do what Jesus calls us to do.

***Acts 10:38* "How God anointed Jesus of Nazareth with the Holy Ghost and with power: Who went about doing good, and healing all that were oppressed of the devil; for God was with him."**

If you notice in this verse, it says that Jesus healed ALL that were oppressed of the devil. I'd really like to know what part of ALL doesn't the church get? It's so plain and clear in the Word, yet so many so- called believers can't or won't see it. The church needs to open it's eyes, and see the truth that is so clearly evident. Let's look at even more verses that plainly show healing and deliverance:

***Luke 4:18-19* "The Spirit of the Lord is upon me, Because He hath anointed me to preach the Gospel to**

the poor; He hath sent me to heal the brokenhearted, to preach deliverance to the captives; and recovering of sight to the blind, to set at liberty them that are bruised, To preach the acceptable year of the Lord."

Mark 6:13 "And they cast out devils, and anointed with oil many that were sick, and healed them."

So remember, just because someone says they are a believer, doesn't mean they truly are - according to God's definition of a believer. As a true believer who is anointed for the battle, we don't have to chase after signs, because the signs are suppose to follow us!

Mark 16:20 "And they went forth, and preached every where, the Lord working with them and confirming the Word with signs following. Amen."

Not only can we do the works and miracles of Jesus, but He said we can do even greater works than those. The reason we can is because we have the Holy Spirit Who anoints us, and lives on the inside of us. He is our Source of spiritual Power. Look at John chapter 14:

***John 14:12* "Verily, verily, I say unto you, he that believeth on me, the works that I do shall he do also; and greater works than these shall he do; because I go unto my Father."**

God the Father is on His Throne in heaven, and Jesus is at His right hand, and the Holy Spirit is on the inside of us, empowering us to do the works of the Lord Jesus. The Holy Spirit is God on the earth, indwelling us - believers, for we are the temple of the Holy Spirit.

John 14:16, 26 "And I will pray the Father, and he shall give you another Comforter, that he may abide with you for ever; Even the Spirit of truth; Whom the world cannot receive, because it seeth him not, neither knoweth him: but ye know him; for he dwelleth with you, and shall be in you."

Verse 26 "But the Comforter, which is the Holy Ghost, Whom the Father will send in my name, he shall teach you all things, and bring all things to your remembrance, whatsoever I have said unto you."

How truly sad it is that so many churches and ministries have neglected the commission from our Lord Jesus to lay hands on the sick. How sad that these professing "believers" want no part of healing and deliverance. The devil has blinded their minds, and is working over-time to discredit the work of the Cross. The old devil knows full well about divine healing, and he will try all he can to try and convince you that it is "God's will for you to be sick". What a lie straight from the very pits of hell itself! God doesn't want you sick. God wants you well. That's how we can testify unto others - by showing them how God heals and sets free. Like I said before, healing is for God's glory. Pain and sickness does not glorify God, it glorifies the devil. I don't care if you don't like to hear that - you're going to hear it anyway! Stop being led astray by false doctrine and the traditions of men. Start following God, and let Him lead you into all truth. Remember, God is the Giver of all good things, and healing is a good thing!

James 1:17 **"Every good gift and every perfect gift is from above, and cometh down from the Father of lights, with whom is no variableness, neither shadow of turning."**

Jeremiah 17:14 **"Heal me, O Lord, and I shall be healed; save me, and I shall be saved: for thou art my praise."**

Like I've said, healing is for God's glory. His healing anointing is available to each of us who are born again. We have the anointing in us, and upon us, and it's up to us to let the anointing flow freely. In the book of Acts we see that the anointing was so strong on Peter, that even his shadow healed people. That's the anointing that destroys every yoke, and removes every burden! Let's take a look at these passages:

Acts 5:12-16 **"And by the hands of the apostles were many signs and wonders wrought among the people; (and they were all with one accord in Solomon's porch. And of the rest durst no man join himself to them: but the people magnified them. And believers were the more added to the**

Lord, multitudes both of men and women.) Insomuch that they brought forth the sick into the streets, and laid them on beds and couches, that at the least the shadow of Peter passing by might overshadow some of them. There came also a multitude out of the cities round about unto Jerusalem, bringing sick folks, and them which were vexed with unclean spirits: and they were healed every one."

Isaiah 10:27 "And it shall come to pass in that day, that his burden shall be taken away from off thy shoulder; and his yolk from off thy neck, and the yolk shall be destroyed because of the anointing."

When was the last time your shadow healed somebody? Just stop and think about it. The very anointed Holy Spirit lives on the inside of born-again believers. We have what this lost and dying world do desperately needs.

There are countless people out there that need healing and restoration. We have the command from Jesus to go forth and heal the sick in His Name. This is not just for a select few. Listen up very closely - THIS IS FOR THE ENTIRE CHURCH! Jesus said that these signs shall follow them that believe - casting out demons, speaking with new tongues, taking up serpents, being unharmed by anything deadly, and laying hands on the sick who shall recover. If you want to call me radical, that's fine. They thought Jesus was radical too, so I am in very good company! You will be too if you choose to obey the great commission that Jesus has given. (Also see **Acts 8:5-8, Acts 9:32-43, Acts 14:8-10, Acts 19:11-12, Acts 28:7-9, Luke 6:17-19, Luke 7:21-22, Luke 8:41-56, Luke 13:10-13, John 5:1-9, Jeremiah 30:17, Isaiah 57:19, Psalms 30:2, Psalms 107:20, Psalms 147:3, Exodus 15:26 b, MalachI 4:2** - for further study on healing).

Now that we have looked at the five signs of the believer, I want to also tell you that God is no respecter of persons.

GOD IS NO RESPECTER OF PERSONS:

Everyone needs to understand that God anoints and appoints both men and women to do the works of Jesus Christ and His kingdom. In Christ Jesus we are all one. God does not look at male or female. God looks at the heart, and He sees us as His very body - the church. Gender and age has nothing at all to do with it. Period. Let's look to the Scriptures:

***Galatians 3:26-28* "For ye are all the children of God by faith in Christ Jesus. For as many of you as have been baptized into Christ have put**

on Christ. There is neither Jew nor Greek, there is neither bond nor free, there is neither male nor female: for ye are all one in Christ Jesus."

Acts 10:34-35 "Then Peter opened his mouth, and said, Of a truth I perceive that God is no respecter of persons: But in every nation he that feareth him, and worketh righteousness, is accepted with him."

Romans 2:11 "For there is no respect of persons with God."

There has been a quite a lot of arguing and debating over whether or not women are called into the ministry. Well, as we have just clearly seen in The Word, God is no respecter of persons. He can use a woman just as He can use a man. As a matter of fact, it was a woman who first told the Good News of Jesus' resurrection. Let's look at the book of Matthew:

Matthew 28:1 "In the end of the Sabbath, as it began to dawn toward the first day of the week, came Mary Magdalene and the other Mary to see the sepulchre."

Matthew 28:5-10 "And the angel answered and said unto the women, Fear not ye: for I know that ye seek Jesus which was crucified. He is not here: for He is risen, as He said. Come, see the place where the Lord lay. And go quickly, and tell his disciples that he is risen from the dead; and behold, He goeth before you into Galilee; there shall ye see him: lo, I have told you. And they departed quickly from the sepulchre with fear and great joy; and did run to bring his disciples word. And as they went to tell his disciples, behold, Jesus met them, saying, All hail. And they came and held Him by the feet, and worshipped Him. Then said Jesus unto them, Be not

afraid: go tell my brethren that they go into Galilee, and there shall they see me."

We see many places in the Bible where God used women in ministry. Many denominational churches have put women into bondage by telling them that God doesn't "allow women to preach or teach in church". How very sad that these so called Christians would forbid women to do something that God doesn't forbid them to do. These so called ministers and believers usually twist a few Scriptures to try and "prove" their position on the matter, but as we shall see, the very Word of God speaks for Himself. Let's now take a look at the two most commonly used Scripture verses that these so called believers like to use to try and "prove" that women are not allowed to preach and teach:

1 Corinthians 14:34-35 **"Let your women keep silence in the churches:**

for it is not permitted unto them to speak; but they are commanded to be under obedience, as also saith the law. And if they will learn anything; let them ask their husbands at home: for it is a shame for women to speak in the church."

1 Timothy 2:11-15 **"Let the woman learn in silence with all subjection. But I suffer not a woman to teach, nor to usurp authority over the man, but to be in silence. For Adam was first formed, then Eve. And Adam was not deceived, but the woman being deceived was in the transgression. Notwithstanding she shall be saved in childbearing, if they continue in faith and charity and holiness with sobriety."**

As you will notice, these two Scripture passages are talking about husbands and wives. You have to understand that in the context of these passages that it's not talking about all women, because not all women have a husband. There are some women who are single. The first passage says **"Let them ask their husbands".** Paul was not talking about all women in these verses. He was talking about wives. Wives are not supposed to dictate and run rough-shod over their husbands. Back in the early Church men usually sat on one side of the church, and the women sat on the other side. So rather than the women screaming to her husband on the other side of the building to ask a question, Paul was telling them to wait until they got home to ask their husbands. That way they wouldn't interrupt the church service, and usurp the preacher's authority. In the second passage from first Timothy - Paul was saying that women are not to usurp the authority over a man. He gives the example of Adam and Eve - where he says that Adam was created first. Now, this does not mean that men are superior to women. It just shows us that God has created men and women differently. This verse in Timothy does not in any way imply that a woman can't teach or preach. People through tradition have kept women from answering the call of God on their lives by misinterpreting the Scriptures. As we have already studied, God is no respecter of persons. We see all throughout the Bible - both Old and New Testaments, where God used women. There was Anna - who was a prophetess (See **Luke 2:36-38**), There was Miriam who was a leader in Israel, a prophetess, and a leader of congregational worship (See **Exodus 15:20-21**, **Micah 6:4**). There was Deborah - who was a judge in Israel, and a prophetess (See **Judges 4:4-24, 5:1-31**). There was Esther - who was placed in a position of influence to further God's plans and purposes (See the book of **Esther**). There was Phoebe, who was a deacon in the church (See **Romans 16:1-2**). And there was also Priscilla, who, along with her husband, led a church in their house, and also helped launch the ministry of Apollos. Let's look at the Scriptures:

Acts 18:24-26 **"And a certain Jew named Apollos, born at Alexandria, an eloquent man, and mighty in the scriptures, came to Ephesus. This man was instructed in the way of the Lord; and being fervent in spirit, he spake and taught diligently the things of the Lord, knowing only the baptism of John. And he began to speak boldly in the synagogue: whom when Aquilla and Priscilla had heard, they took him unto them, and expounded unto him the way of God more perfectly. And when he was disposed to pass into Achaia, the brethren wrote, exhorting the disciples to receive him: who, when he was come, helped them much which had believed through grace: For he mightily convinced the Jews, and that publicly, shewing by the scriptures that Jesus was Christ."

Romans 16:3-5 "Greet Priscilla and Aquila my helpers in Christ Jesus: Who have for my life laid down their own necks: unto whom not only I give thanks, but also all the churches of the Gentiles. Likewise greet the church that is in their house. Salute my well beloved Epaenetus, who is the first fruits of Achaia unto Christ."

1 Corinthians 16:19 "The churches of Asia salute you. Aquila and Priscilla salute you much in the Lord, with the church that is in their house."

Another passage of Scripture that I want us to take a look at and study, is from the book of Psalms:

Psalms 68:11 "The Lord gave the word: great was the company of those that published it."

Now let's take a look at this same Scripture verse in *The Amplified Bible* to see the Hebrew and Greek meanings brought out:

Psalms 68:11 "The Lord gives the word [of power]; the women who bear and publish (the news) are a great host."

(The Amplified Bible)

Our God is no respecter of persons, and He has given both men and women the great commission to go forth and give witness of the Good News of the Gospel. It's the Lord God Who gives us the Word of power, and we are to go forth and do what He has commanded us. Don't be held back by the vain traditions of men. Take hold of the Word of God, and start walking in your full authority and position in Christ Jesus!

Mark 16:20 "And they went forth, and preached every where, the Lord working with them, and confirming the Word with signs following. Amen."

The Holy Spirit is our Teacher, and He will empower us to walk in our authority. He will empower us to be more than conquerors, more than overcomers who run the race to win. So don't give up or lose heart, stand up strong dressed in your armor, wielding your divine weapons, and march forth as God's anointed. Be one that hears "Well done, good and faithful servant (son)"

1 Corinthians 9:24-27 "**Know ye not that they which run in a race run all, but one receiveth the prize? So run, that ye may obtain. And every man that striveth for the mastery is temperate in all things. Now they do**

it to obtain a corruptible crown; but we an incorruptible. I therefore so run, not as uncertainly; so fight I, not as one that beateth the air: But I keep under my body, and bring it into subjection: lest that by any means, when I have preached to others, I myself should be a castaway."

In a natural race, the competitors are competing for a prize such as a trophy or a ribbon. In the supernatural race, we as Christians are running a race where the prize at the end is one that will never tarnish, or fade, or corrupt. Jesus is our Coach cheering us on, and telling us don't give up, keep running, and overcome!

Hebrews 12:1-2 **"Wherefore seeing we also are compassed about with so great a cloud of witnesses, let us lay aside every weight, and the sin which doth so easily beset us, and let us run with patience the race that is** set before us, Looking unto Jesus the author and finisher of our faith; Who for the joy that was set before him endured the Cross, despising the shame, and is set down at the right hand of the throne of God."

Galatians 6:9 "And let us not be weary in well doing: for in due season we shall reap, if we faint not."

1 John 5:4 "For whatsoever is born of God overcometh the world: and this is the victory that overcometh the world, even our faith."

Revelation 3:21 "To him that overcometh will I grant to sit with me in my throne, even as I also overcame, and am set down with my Father in his throne."

To the believer who overcomes, Jesus said that they would be granted to sit with Him on His throne. On this glorious throne we will be ruling and reigning over the nations as kingdom government. The key to being victorious and finishing the race is to be an overcomer who walks and lives by faith, and who loves Christ's appearing. That's who Jesus is coming back for. Those who are looking for Him. Don't be left behind. Choose today to lay hold on eternal life in Christ Jesus.

1 Timothy 6:12 **"Fight the good fight of faith, lay hold on eternal life, whereunto thou art also called, and hast professed a good profession before many witnesses."**

2 Timothy 4:7-8 **"I have fought a good fight, I have finished my course, I have kept the faith: Henceforth there is laid up for me a crown of righteousness, which the Lord, the righteous judge shall give me at that Day: and not to me only, but unto all them also that love his**

appearing."

A crown of righteousness is given to all those who finish the race, and who love Jesus' appearing. This is in reference to the Rapture of the Church, which is Pre-Tribulation. This is the next big event on God's time-table of last days events. We know the Rapture is pre-tribulation because God reserves wrath for His enemies, and the anointed Church is not an enemy, but His very Body. Let's look at this in The Word:

Nahum 1:2 **"God is jealous, and the Lord revengeth; the Lord revengeth, and is furious; the Lord will take vengeance on his adversaries, and he reserves wrath for his enemies."**

1 Thessalonians 1:10 **"And to wait for his Son from heaven, whom he raised from the dead, even Jesus, which delivered us from the wrath to come."**

1 Thessalonians 5:9 "For God hath not appointed us to wrath, but to obtain salvation by our Lord Jesus Christ."

Romans 5:8-9 "But God commendeth his love toward us, in that, while we were yet sinners, Christ died for us. Much more then, being now justified by his blood, we shall be saved from wrath through him. For if, when we were enemies, we were reconciled to God by the death of his Son, much more, being reconciled, we shall be saved by his life."

God is going to pour out His wrath during the tribulation, and this is for all those who reject Him. The body of Christ - the anointed Church, will not be here, glory to God ! We are the restraining force that holds the antichrist back. Once we, the Church are taken out of the way - (the Rapture), then the antichrist will rise to power here on earth - signaling the beginning of the seven year tribulation period. Like I said, we will not be here. (See **2 Thessalonians 2:1-14**).

1 Thessalonians 4:16-18 **" For the Lord himself shall descend from heaven with a shout, with the voice of the archangel, and with the trump of God: and the dead in Christ shall rise first: Then we which are alive and remain shall be caught up together with them in the clouds, to meet the Lord in the air: and so shall we ever be with the Lord. Wherefore comfort one another with these words."**

Praise God, we can exhort one another with these comforting words because we have eternity with the Lord in heaven. We were counted worthy to escape all the horrors that will befall this world once the tribulation begins. Choose to be a part of Christ's body now. Choose to hear "come up hither" once that last trump sounds, and eternity begins!

***Revelation 4:1* "After this I looked, and, behold, a door was opened in heaven: and the first voice which I heard was as it were of a trumpet talking with me; which said, come up hither, and I will shew thee things which must be hereafter."**

So don't put it off any longer. If you do, you might find yourself caught in the middle of the tribulation. Choose today to love His awesome appearance!

So, if we want to be the true body of Christ now, and for all eternity, then we had better know how to walk the Christian walk. We better know our weapons and how to use them against the devil and his cohorts. We must know and use our God given authority as believers in Christ Jesus. There's no room for lazy soldiers in the army of

God. Without knowing and using your authority, the enemy can run roughshod over you, and talk you out of your place in the Rapture. We will look more at the Rapture later in this book, but right now we need to look at the authority we have as believers.

THE AUTHORITY OF THE BELIEVER:

Luke 10:19 **"Behold, I give unto you power to tread on serpents and scorpions, and over all the power of the enemy: and nothing shall by any means hurt you."**

We have been delegated power and authority over the devil and his kingdom of darkness. We have the Name of Jesus, we have the power of the blood, the power of The Word, and we have the Holy Spirit. We need to learn to use our God given authority every single day. We looked at the signs of the believer earlier, now we need to take ground. We need to do damage in the devil's kingdom. We as Christians have authority over demons, over sickness and diseases, over lack, over sin, over the weather, and over the devil himself. We are called, and appointed, and anointed for the battle that is before us. That is a part of our position in Christ.

AUTHORITY OVER DEMONS:

Mark 3:13-15 **"And he goeth up into a mountain, and calleth unto him whom he would: and they came unto him. And he ordained twelve, that they should be with him, and that he might send them forth to preach, and to have power to heal sicknesses, and to cast out devils."**

Acts 16:16-18 **"And it came to pass, as we went to prayer, a certain damsel possessed with a spirit of divination met us, which brought her masters much gain by**

soothsaying: The same followed Paul and us, and cried, saying, These men are the servants of the most high God, which shew unto us the way of salvation. And this did she many days. But Paul, being grieved, turned and said to the spirit, I command thee in the name of Jesus Christ to come out of her. And he came out the same hour."

We don't have to put up with foul demon spirits harassing us, we have the authority in Jesus Name to cast them out. Don't be a whiny Christian, intimidated by a lying demon. Stand up boldly against that thing, and use the authority that Jesus Christ has given you as one of His representatives. Demons have to bow at the Name of Jesus, and they have to bow to you because you are coming in the Name of Jesus. Remember, it's not our name that they bow to, it's the Name of Jesus.

AUTHORITY OVER SICKNESS AND DISEASE:

Acts 3:2-8 "And a certain man lame from his mother's womb was carried, whom they laid daily at the gate of the temple which is called Beautiful, to ask alms of them that entered into the temple; who seeing Peter and John about to go into the temple asked an alms. And Peter, fastening his eyes upon him with John, said, Look on us. And he gave heed unto them, expecting to receive something of them. Then Peter said, Silver and gold have I none; but such as I have give I thee: In the name of Jesus Christ of Nazareth rise up and walk. And he took him by the right hand, and lifted him up; and immediately his feet and ankle bones received strength. And he leaping up stood, and walked, and entered with them into the temple, walking, and leaping, and praising God."

Peter and John knew the power of the Name of Jesus, and they knew they had authority over infirmities and sickness, so they exercised their authority - and the lame man was restored back to health, to the glory of God. As we looked at earlier, sickness and disease does not glorify God. Being healed and made whole glorifies God. Remember, Jesus said that believers would lay hands on the sick, and they would recover. (See **Mark 16:18, James 5:13-16**).

AUTHORITY OVER THE WEATHER:

Mark 4:35-41 **"And the same day, when the even was come, he saith unto them, Let us pass over unto the other side. And when they had sent away the multitude, they took him even as he was in the ship. And there were also with him other little ships. And there arose a great storm of**

wind, and the waves beat into the ship, so that it was now full. And he was in the hinder part of the ship, asleep on a pillow: and they awake him, and say unto him, Master, carest thou not that we perish? And he arose, and rebuked the wind, and said unto the sea, Peace, be still. And the wind ceased, and there was a great calm. And he said unto them, why are ye so fearful? How is it that ye have no faith? And they feared exceedingly, and said one to another, what manner of man is this, that even the wind and the sea obey him?"

Jesus spoke to the wind and the sea and said peace be still - and it did because of His authority over it. Just like Jesus, we can speak to the storms and take authority over them. Tornadoes, hurricanes, or whatever kind of storm - command it to be still in Jesus Name. Just like we can speak to the mountains in our lives, we can speak to the storms no matter what kind they are. We see in verse 41 that they were amazed at His authority, but they didn't realize that they had the same authority. If only they would have stepped out in faith, and exercised their authority, they too could have spoken to the weather.

AUTHORITY OVER LACK:

Psalms 34:9-10 **"O fear the Lord, ye his saints, for there is no want to them that fear him. The young lions do lack, and suffer hunger, but they that seek the Lord shall not want any good thing."**

Psalms 23:1 **"The Lord is my shepherd; I shall not want."**

Philippians 4:19 **"But my God shall supply all your need according to his riches in glory by Christ Jesus."**

Like I said earlier, Jesus took poverty

on the Cross. We don't have to want for anything. We serve a good God Who provides for our needs. Lack and poverty are curses from the devil, and we as believers have authority over it. Believers everywhere need to speak to lack and command it to break it's hold off. God desires that His children prosper. God is the All Sufficient One - El-Shaddai. He's Jehovah-Jireh - The Lord our Provider. It's up to us to take authority over lack and poverty, and bind it in the Name of Jesus.

***3 John 2* "Beloved, I wish above all things that thou mayest prosper and be in health, even as thy soul prospereth."**

***Psalms 68:19* "Blessed be the Lord, who daily loadeth us with benefits, even the God of our salvation."**

***Psalms 37:25* "I have been young, and now am old; yet have I not seen the righteous forsaken, nor his seed**

begging bread."

***Psalms 118:25* "Save now, I beseech thee, O Lord: O Lord, I beseech thee, send now prosperity."**

All these passages of Scripture clearly show us that poverty and lack are not for us. These Scriptures show us that God delights in prospering His children. God daily loads us with benefits and blessings. In fact, God showers us with blessings. It's up to us to receive them, and to not let the devil steal from us. We have authority in the Name of Jesus to send "lack" & "poverty" back to the pit where it belongs!

***Ezekiel 34:26* "And I will make them and the places round about my hill a blessing; and I will cause the shower to come down in his season; there shall be showers of blessing."**

AUTHORITY OVER SIN:

Romans 6:6, 12-14, 17-18 "Knowing this, that our old man is crucified with him, that the body of sin might be destroyed, that henceforth we should not serve sin."

Verses 12-14 "Let not sin therefore reign in your mortal body, that ye should obey it in the lusts thereof. Neither yield ye your members as instruments of unrighteousness unto sin: but yield yourselves unto God, as those that are alive from the dead, and your members as instruments of righteousness unto God. For sin shall not have dominion over you: for ye are not under the law, but under grace."

Verses 17-18 "But God be thanked, that ye were the servants of sins, but ye have obeyed from the heart that form of doctrine which was delivered you. Being then made free from sin, ye became the servants of

righteousness."

Sin doesn't have to have authority over us. We are to have authority over it. All unrighteousness is sin, and Jesus has well equipped us with the authority to defeat every contrary thing that opposes God's holy kingdom - and sin is one of them. Jesus said that if we would confess our sins, that He would be faithful and forgive us, and cleanse us from all unrighteousness. That's how good our God is. He faithfully forgives us every sin and iniquity. Our job is to confess them, and forsake them. Don't let the devil put condemnation upon you. Talk right back at that old lying serpent and let him know who you are in Christ. Let him know that sin won't have any dominion over you. Use your rightful authority over sin, and let Christ cleanse you with His precious blood.

***1 John 1:9* "If we confess our sins, He is faithful and just to forgive us**

our sins, and to cleanse us from all unrighteousness."

Romans 8:1 "There is therefore now no condemnation to them which are in Christ Jesus, who walk not after the flesh, but after the Spirit."

Start walking in the Spirit, and learn to take authority over sin before it takes authority over you.

AUTHORITY OVER THE DEVIL:

James 4:7 "Submit yourselves therefore to God. Resist the devil, and he will flee from you."

The way a Christian resists the devil is by being fully submitted unto God. This is cause and effect. If we want to successfully resist the enemy and take all authority over him, we are going to have to be submitted to Almighty God, and His precious Word - and God and His Word are One and the same. We are to imitate our Example - Jesus Christ, and walk as He walked, and that includes doing the things that He did - taking authority over demons, sickness, lack, the weather, sin, and the devil.

***1 John 2:6* "He that saith he abideth in him ought himself also so to walk, even as he walked."**

***1 John 4:17* "Herein is our love made perfect, that we may have boldness in the day of judgment: because as He is, so are we in this world."**

Jesus didn't just tip-toe through the tulips - He was a warrior, He came to set the captives free, and He came to destroy the works of the devil. (See **Luke 4:18, Acts 10:38, 1 John 3:8**). Christians need to learn to talk back to the devil like Jesus did, and tell him - IT IS WRITTEN ! Use the Sword of the Spirit against the devil and his nasty demons. When the devil came to tempt Jesus in the wilderness, this is what Jesus told him:

Matthew 4:4 **"But he answered and said, It is written, man shall not live by bread alone, but by every Word that proceedeth out of the mouth of God."**

Don't be wimpy and whiny. Have demanding authority. The devil needs to know we mean business. When we demand our rights, were not demanding of God, we are demanding of the devil. Were telling the devil to give it up in Jesus Name. That's the kind of authority we have as Christians. Demanding authority over all the works of the devil. It doesn't matter what trick he pulls, we have the Holy Spirit on the inside of us - Who is greater and mightier than the devil. We have the very command of Jesus our King - to do the work of the kingdom - which includes taking our rightful authority as believers. Let's look at a passage from the book of Matthew:

Matthew 28:18-20 **"And Jesus came and spake unto them, saying, All power is given unto me in heaven and in earth. Go ye therefore, and teach all nations, baptizing them in the name of the Father, and of the Son, and of the Holy Ghost; teaching them to observe all things whatsoever I have commanded you: and lo, I am with you always, even unto the end of the world. Amen."**

We are the body of Christ - and Jesus has conferred His authority on the earth to us. So if problems exist, it's because we have allowed them to, and haven't taken authority over them. Don't be a passive Christian, stand up and take action. We are a part of God's Swat Team - His anointed Remnant that is as bold as a lion. There's no place for cowards or sissies in this army. Stand up, and be counted!

Proverbs 28:1 "**The wicked flee when no man pursueth: but the righteous are bold as a lion.**"

Don't fear the enemy or those whom he uses against you. As a believer, you have a heritage in Christ, which includes divine protection from the enemy's weapons.

Isaiah 54:17 "**No weapon that is formed against thee shall prosper; and every tongue that shall rise against thee in judgment thou shalt condemn. This is the heritage of the servants of the Lord, and their righteousness is of me, saith the Lord.**"

Lift up your shield of faith, and when you do, the darts of the devil will be of no effect. No weapon formed against you will prosper. No tongue of judgment, or defeat can attach to you. No tongue of sickness, or lack, or oppression can attach to you. You are covered by the very blood of Jesus, and you can condemn every attack of the devil. Those that want God's anointing upon them have to take a stand for Christ and not be concerned with what people say or think. Like we looked at earlier, the righteous are bold as a lion. Stand up and call sin - sin. Stand up and call abortion what it is - murder. One of the things God hates is **"….hands that shed innocent blood" (Proverbs 6:17)**. Abortion is a foul spirit of death, and the devil - the thief, is the author of it. Life begins at conception, and God is all about life, and life more abundantly.

Exodus 20:13 **"Thou shalt not kill."**

John 10:10 **"The thief cometh not, but for to steal, and to kill, and to destroy: I am come that they might have life, and that they might have it more abundantly."**

Psalms 127:3 "Lo, children are an heritage of the Lord: and the fruit of the womb is his reward."

Jeremiah 1:4-5 **"Then the word of the Lord came unto me, saying, Before I formed thee in the belly I knew thee; and before thou camest forth out of the womb I sanctified thee, and I ordained thee a prophet unto the nations."**

Stand up and choose to be Pro-Life, not pro-choice - which is really pro-death, to be very blunt and straightforward. Stand up and call homosexuality what it is - a foul spirit, a perversion and an abomination. Marriage was created by God to be between one man, and one woman. Anything else is sin and will be judged by God.

Leviticus 18:22 **"Thou shalt not lie with mankind, as with womankind: it is abomination."**

Romans 1:26-27 "For this cause God gave them up unto vile affections: for even their women did change the natural use into that which is against nature; And likewise also the men, leaving the natural use of the woman, burned in their lust one toward another; men with men working that which is unseemly, and receiving in themselves that recompence of their error which was meet."

1 Corinthians 6:9-10 "Know ye not that the unrighteous shall not inherent the kingdom of God? Be not deceived: neither fornicators, nor idolaters, nor adulterers, nor effeminate, nor abusers of themselves with mankind, Nor thieves, nor covetous, nor drunkards, nor revilers, nor extortioners, shall inherit the kingdom of God."

Dare to be controversial. Jesus was controversial, and He didn't care one bit what people thought of Him. He did what pleased the Father, not man. If you are persecuted for standing up for what is right, then bless God, you are doing what Jesus did, so you are in very good company. Don't fret, just rejoice! - your heavenly reward is greater than any temporary praise of men. Don't be concerned with your "reputation". Jesus made Himself of no reputation (See **Philippians 2:7**). There's far too many wimpy preachers who are more concerned with filling their Church pews, than with seeing people filled with the truth. They're more concerned with filling their wallets, than seeing people saved and born again. So called "preachers" that go on television and don't have the backbone to stand up for what is right, and call sin - sin. They're afraid they might offend someone. Well, I got news for you, you will, but so did Jesus. Stand up for the Gospel, and don't compromise. When you compromise the Word of God, you open up a door for the devil. Let's take a look at a few Scriptures:

Matthew 5:10-12 **"Blessed are they which are persecuted for righteousness sake: for theirs is the kingdom of heaven. Blessed are ye, when men shall revile you, and persecute you, and shall say all manner of evil against you falsely, for my sake. Rejoice, and be exceeding glad for great is your reward in heaven: for so persecuted they the prophets which were before you."**

2 Timothy 3:12 **"Yea, and all that will live godly in Christ Jesus shall suffer persecution."**

1 Peter 4:16 **"Yet if any man suffer as a Christian, let him not be ashamed; but let him glorify God on this behalf."**

1 John 3:13 "Marvel not, my brethren, if the world hate you."

Romans 1:16 "For I am not ashamed of the Gospel of Christ: for it is the power of God unto salvation to every one that believeth; to the Jew first, and also to the Greek."

The true body of Christ is peculiar to those who are outside. God made it that way. We are new creatures, God's royal priesthood. We are His special people, anointed by the Holy Spirit to be the light and salt of the earth. That's a part of our heritage in Christ. We have been made new in Him, called forth to proclaim His marvelous praises.

1 Peter 2:9-10 "But ye are a chosen generation, a royal priesthood, an holy nation, a peculiar people; that ye should shew forth the praises of Him who hath called you out of darkness into his marvelous light: Which in time past were not a people, but are now the people of God: Which had not obtained mercy, but now have obtained mercy."

We are not the same people anymore, praise God. We are saved, born again, devil stomping warriors anointed for battle. We are the sons of obedience. Which brings me to the next thing I want us to look at.

EXPOSING WITCHCRAFT AND THE OCCULT:

We just read where the Lord has called us out of darkness into His light. It always amazes me, and has for many years, how many Christians see no problem dabbling in things that pertain to the Occult and witchcraft. Let me tell you, these things are not just innocent fun. These things are from the devil, and they give him and his demons legal right to destroy you. As Christians we are not to have anything to do with the darkness. We are to expose witchcraft and the occult in all it's forms. Whether it's overtly occultic, or even subtle, it is to be exposed and renounced. Quija boards, tarot cards, horoscopes, zodiac, magic, E.s.p., yoga, martial-arts, dream catchers, statues of false gods, Virgin Mary statues, statues of beggars, geisha-girls, yin-yang symbols, owls, frogs, unicorns, heavy metal/hard rock records & tapes, gargoyles, wizards, dragons, fortune tellers, psychics, hypnotism, superstitions, acupuncture, free-masonry, Pokemon, Harry-Potter, Star-Wars, reincarnation, horror movies, etc. All these things are of the occult or New-age, and must be avoided. Christians need to do spiritual housecleaning, and remove anything that promotes witchcraft or the New-age, or a false religion or practice. Foul spirits attach themselves to objects that glorify or promote Satan and his kingdom. Christians have no business watching horror movies, or celebrating abominations like Halloween and St. Patrick's Day. Halloween is a celebration of death and destruction, and all evil, and we know who authors that - the devil. St. Patrick's Day involves leprechauns which are demons, and so called luck. Well, there is no such thing as luck, good or bad. Either you are blessed, or you're not. Luck is involved with superstitions, which is all a part of the devil's agenda. Santa Claus and the Easter Bunny are also to be avoided as they promote lies and idolatry. Just think about it, all you have to do is change the letters around in SANTA, and guess what it spells? This is not coincidence, this is a part of Satan's agenda. Santa along with the Easter bunny, are high things that exalt themselves against the knowledge of God. (See **2 Corinthians 10:5**). As Christians, we are called to be light, not darkness, so don't partake of the darkness, instead expose it.

Ephesians 5:6-13 **"Let no man deceive you with vain words: for because of these things cometh the wrath of God upon the children of disobedience. Be not ye therefore partakers with them. For ye were sometimes darkness, but now are ye light in the Lord: walk as children of light: (For the fruit of the Spirit is in all goodness and righteousness and truth); Proving what is acceptable unto the Lord. And have no fellowship with the unfruitful works of darkness, but rather reprove them. For it is a shame even to speak of those things which are done of them in secret. But all things that are reproved are made manifest by the light: for whatsoever doth make manifest is light."**

1 Thessalonians 5:22 **"Abstain from all appearance of evil."**

God makes it very clear in His Word that we are to have nothing to do with occult practices of any kind. Let's look at Deuteronomy.

Deuteronomy 18:9-14 **"When thou art come into the land which the Lord thy God giveth thee, thou shalt not learn to do after the abominations of those nations. There shall not be found among you any one that maketh his son or his daughter to pass through the fire, or that useth divination, or an observer of times, or an enchanter, or a witch, or a charmer, or a consulter with familiar spirits, or a wizard, or a necromancer. For all that do these things are an abomination unto the Lord: and because of these abominations the Lord thy God doth drive them out from before thee. Thou shalt be perfect with the Lord thy God. For these nations, which thou shalt possess, hearkened unto** observers of times, and unto diviners: but as for thee, the Lord thy God hath not suffered thee so to do."

Leviticus 19:31 "Regard not them that have familiar spirits, neither seek after wizards, to be defiled by them: I am the Lord your God."

Christians have no business going to fortune-tellers and psychics. Our conversation is in heaven, not in the lake of fire. God has a future for us, and we don't need to seek guidance from someone like a psychic who is getting their information from a demon. Also stay away from zodiacs and horoscopes. If you want to know your future, get into God's Word. Get into His presence and you can find out what God wants for your life. Believe me, He knows what is best for us. God has a wonderful plan for each of us. Read the Book.

Jeremiah 29:11 **"For I know the thoughts that I think toward you, says the Lord, thoughts of peace and not of evil, to give you a future and a hope."**
(NKJV)

There is also a lot of so called Christian movies and media that is laden with witchcraft and the occult. We must not watch or participate in any of it. Doing so brings a curse, and legal ground for the enemy. It doesn't matter how "little" the occult content is, we still must avoid it, and call it what it is - evil. Don't ever compromise. Compromise will open the door for the devil every time. We must stand firm upon the Word of God.

Isaiah 5:20 **"Woe unto them that call evil good, and good evil; that put darkness for light, and light for darkness; that put bitter for sweet, and sweet for bitter!"**

Psalms 97:10 **"Ye that love the Lord, hate evil: he preserveth the souls of his saints; he delivereth them out of the hand of the wicked."**

Romans 13:12 **"The night is far spent, the day is at hand: let us therefore cast off the works of darkness, and let us put on the armour of light."**

Anyone participating or accepting the occult and witchcraft in any form, is operating in a spirit of rebellion. The Word of God says that rebellion is as the sin of witchcraft. Let's look at 1 Samuel chapter 15:

1 Samuel 15:23 **"For rebellion is as the sin of witchcraft, and stubbornness is as iniquity and idolatry. Because thou hast rejected the word of the Lord, he hath also rejected thee from being king."**

If you have participated in any occult practices, or New-age practices, repent, and renounce them, and anoint your home with oil - as a symbol of the Holy Spirit, as a protective covering. Remove all objects including books and music, and any media that is of the occult, new age, or false religions, and destroy those cursed items. This also includes demonic jewelry such as the Egyptian ankh, pentagrams, hexagrams, the horned star, and any other jewelry that has occult symbols on them. Also, the "star of David" is another idolatrous occult symbol that needs to be avoided. It is not the symbol of Israel as so many ignorantly believe and promote. It's a six pointed star that is formed by two triangles (hexagram), and belongs to the star god named Saturn, who also goes by the name Remphan. (See **Acts 7:41-43**). This symbol has nothing whatsoever to do with David. It's time that Christians start being discerning and on their toes regarding these things. We must not give the devil any entrance in our lives in any way, shape, or form. Let's now read in the books of Deuteronomy & Acts, as we continue to expose witchcraft and the occult:

Deuteronomy 7:25-26 **"The graven images of their gods shall ye burn with fire: thou shalt not desire the silver or gold that is on them, nor take it unto thee, lest thou be snared therein: for it is an abomination to the Lord thy God. Neither shalt thou bring an abomination into thine house, lest thou be a cursed thing like it: but thou shalt utterly detest it, and thou shalt utterly abhor it, for it is a cursed thing."**

Acts 19:19-20 **"Many of them also which used curious arts brought their books together, and burned them before all men: and they counted the price of them, and found it fifty thousand pieces of**

silver. So mightily grew the Word of God and prevailed."

The Word of God prevails in the life of the believer when the accursed thing is removed. Curses are not just limited to objects, they also are attached to places - like land, houses and other buildings where any form of evil has taken place. Curses come in the form of Generational curses, regional curses, and negative words spoken over someone or in a situation. Through the blood of Christ, and the anointing of the Holy Spirit, the believer can get free and stay free. The key is to cut off the curse and the assignment from satan, and start walking in the light of Christ. To successfully demolish strongholds and cut off assignments and curses, you have to identify it, cancel it, and cut it off at the root. I mentioned negative words spoken earlier. Words are containers for power - both positive, and negative.

THE POWER OF YOUR WORDS:

Proverbs 18:21 **"Death and life are in the power of the tongue: and they that love it shall eat the fruit thereof."**

We are either going to eat the good fruit of life, or the rotten fruit of death. Phrases such as "Oh that just kills me", "Oh that just tickles me to death", and the like, should never come out of your mouth. Repeatedly speaking death filled words brings a curse on your life - an open door for the devil. We really need to watch what we say. Our words need to line up with the Word of God.

Proverbs 21:23 **"Whoso keepeth his mouth and his tongue keepeth his soul from troubles."**

Matthew 12:36-37 **"But I say unto you, That every idle word that men shall speak, they shall give account thereof in the day of judgment. For**

by thy words thou shalt be justified, and by thy words thou shalt be condemned."

This also includes profanity. Profanity should never come out of your mouth. It amazes me that there are Christians who don't think anything of it to curse here and there. As far as I'm concerned, it is a bad witness and leaves the door wide open for Satan to take advantage. When you give the enemy an inch, he becomes a ruler. And just to be very blunt, Christians who cuss need to have their mouths washed out with soap. How about some washing of the water of God's Word?

Colossians 3:8 **"But now ye also put off all these; anger, wrath, malice, blasphemy, filthy communication out of your mouth."**

Ephesians 4:29 **"Let no corrupt communication proceed out of your** mouth, but that which is good to the use of edifying, that it may minister grace unto the hearers."

1 Peter 1:13-16 "Wherefore gird up the loins of your mind, be sober, and hope to the end for the grace that is to be brought unto you at the revelation of Jesus Christ; As obedient children, not fashioning yourselves according to the former lusts in your ignorance: But as he which hath called you is holy, so be ye holy in all manner of conversation; Because it is written, Be ye holy, For I am holy."

1 Thessalonians 4:7 "For God hath not called us unto uncleanness, but unto holiness."

We are to walk in holiness, and have conversation that is Christ-like, and Christ-filled. The words we speak need to be words of faith. We have what we say, so we better say the right things.

Like I said, words are containers for power. Both positive and negative. Let's look now at the book of Mark:

Mark 11:12-14, 20-26 "And on the morrow, when they were come from Bethany, he was hungry: And seeing a fig tree afar off having leaves, he came, if haply he might find anything thereon: and when he came to it, he found nothing but leaves; for the time of figs was not yet. And Jesus answered and said unto it, No man eat fruit of thee hereafter for ever. And his disciples heard it."

Verses 20-26 "And in the morning as they passed by, they saw the fig tree dried up from the roots. And Peter calling to remembrance saith unto him, Master, behold, the fig tree which thou cursedst is withered away. And Jesus answering saith unto them, Have faith in God. For verily I say unto you, That whosoever shall say unto this mountain, Be thou removed, and be thou cast into the sea; and shall not doubt in his heart, but shall believe that those things which he saith shall come to pass; he shall have whatsoever he saith. Therefore I say unto you, What things soever ye desire, when ye pray, believe that ye receive them, and ye shall have them. And when ye stand praying, forgive, if ye have ought against any: that your Father also which is in heaven may forgive you your trespasses. But if ye do not forgive, neither will your Father which is in heaven forgive your trespasses."

Jesus cursed the fig tree because it didn't bear any fruit, only leaves. The next morning they passed by the same fig tree, and saw it dried up from the roots. Jesus told the disciples to have faith in God. That means have the God kind of faith. The faith that believes in the heart and speaks with the mouth.

As believers, we can speak to the mountains that are in our way. If we don't doubt, but believe, we will have what we say. Whosoever will have whatsoever if we don't doubt, but truly believe and speak it forth. If you doubt in your heart, then don't speak it with your mouth. Doubt is unbelief, and like all negative words, it will produce havoc in your life. When you pray, believe that what you are praying will come to pass, and it will. Stop speaking the problem, and start speaking and praying the answer. Our confession needs to be a faith confession. Confession brings possession. (See **Hebrews 10:23**). Also remember that in order for our faith to activate properly, we need to be walking in love. Faith works by love. These two spiritual forces go hand in hand like a baseball and a glove. Un-forgiveness will stop the flow of faith in your life just as much as negative words. Let's continue now in the Scriptures:

Galatians 5:6 "For in Jesus Christ neither circumcision availeth anything, nor uncircumcision; but faith which worketh by love."

1 Corinthians 13:2 "And though I have the gift of prophecy, and understand all mysteries and all knowledge, and though I have all faith, so that I could remove mountains, but have not love, I am nothing."
                        (NKJV)

Choose to speak God's Word, because His Word is life and health to us. Our words need to always be acceptable in the sight of God. That has to be in the very forefront of our thinking - being pleasing unto God in our hearts, and in our conversation.

Psalms 19:14 "Let the words of my

mouth, and the meditation of my heart, be acceptable in thy sight, O Lord, my strength, and my redeemer."

Proverbs 4:20-22 **"My son, attend to my words; incline thine ear unto my sayings. Let them not depart from thine eyes; Keep them in the midst of thine heart. For they are life unto those that find them, and health to all their flesh."**

Not only do we need to choose our words wisely, we also need to be wise in those with whom we choose to fellowship. It's one thing to witness to someone, but it's another story when it comes to having a deep fellowship with them. Foul spirits can transfer from them to you. The Word of God tells us not to have fellowship with darkness. We are not to put up with it in any way, shape, or form. We are to expose the darkness, and flee from it. The Bible clearly tells us not to be unequally yoked together with unbelievers. Let's read a few Scripture passages:

2 Corinthians 6:14-18 **"Be ye not unequally yoked together with unbelievers: for what fellowship hath righteousness with unrighteousness? And what communion hath light with darkness? And what concord hath Christ with Belial? Or what part hath he that believeth with an infidel? And what agreement hath the temple of God with idols? For ye are the temple of the living God; as God hath said, I will dwell in them, and walk in them; and I will be their God, and they shall be my people. Wherefore come out from among them, and be ye separate, saith the Lord, and touch not the unclean thing; and I will receive you, And will be a Father unto you, and ye shall be my sons and daughters, saith the Lord Almighty."**

Ephesians 5:11 "And have no fellowship with the unfruitful works of darkness, but rather expose them."
                    (NKJV)

James 4:4 "Ye adulterers and adulteresses, know ye not that the friendship of the world is enmity with God? Whosoever therefore will be a friend of the world is the enemy of God."

1 Corinthians 10:20-21 "But I say, that the things which the Gentiles sacrifice, they sacrifice to devils, and not to God: and I would not that ye should have fellowship with devils. Ye cannot drink the cup of the Lord, and the cup of devils: ye cannot be partakers of the Lord's table, and of the table of devils."

We were once darkness, now we are light in the Lord Jesus. Don't think you can go back to your old stomping grounds and hang around your old friends and not be affected. Think again. Like I said, spirits can transfer from person to person. If we want the anointing of God upon our lives then we better only have fellowship with believers of like precious faith - those who are on the same spiritual page as we are. Unhealthy soul-ties must also be severed. This is essential , if we truly want to walk in the full depth, and measure of God's kingdom. Take a look at Psalms chapter 1:

Psalms 1:1-3 **"Blessed is the man that walketh not in the counsel of the ungodly, nor standeth in the way of sinners, nor sitteth in the seat of the scornful. But his delight is in the law of the Lord; and in his law doth he meditate day and night. And he shall be like a tree planted by the rivers of water, that bringeth forth his fruit in his season; his leaf also shall not wither ;and whatsoever he**

doeth shall prosper."

Don't take counsel from an unbeliever or even a so called believer who doesn't walk in God's Truth. We must be very wise about with whom we share the things of God with. We are definitely to witness Christ to all. Absolutely. No question about that. But the deeper things of God's kingdom are to be shared only with those who are of like precious faith. Those who are in the body of Christ.

Matthew 7:6 **"Give not that which is holy unto the dogs, neither cast ye your pearls before swine, lest they trample them under their feet, and turn again and rend you."**

Philippians 3:2 **"Beware of dogs, beware of evil workers, beware of the concision."**

Don't cast your pearls of God's wisdom before swine. Don't lay out the holy and sacred things for anyone just to come along and trample upon. The enemy's agenda is to use whomever he can to try and discourage and talk us out of what we believe. Unbelievers and many so called believers don't have ears to hear. We can show them the Word of God, but it is up to them to receive it. Like the old saying goes, you can lead a horse to water, but you can't make him drink.

Matthew 13:45-46 **"Again the kingdom of heaven is like unto a merchant man, seeking goodly pearls: who when he had found one pearl of great price, went and sold all that he had, and bought it."**

The anointing, God's Word, the revelations He has given us - these are costly, and we must guard these precious pearls of great price. Just think about it: a natural pearl is very rare, and very costly. How much more costly are the things of God? The pearls of God's kingdom are worth more than anything in this world. Christians must be on their guard. We must be walking the walk, and have our lives filled with the power of the Holy Spirit. If you leave an open door, or even a crack open for the enemy, then he can bring seven more deadly spirits, and it will be even worse than it was before because now you have eight of them to deal with. Look at Luke chapter 11:

Luke 11:24-26 **"When the unclean spirit is gone out of a man, he walketh through dry places, seeking rest; and finding none, he saith, I will return unto my house whence I came out. And when he cometh, he find-eth it swept and garnished. Then goeth he, and taketh to him seven other spirits more wicked than himself; and they enter in, and dwell there: and the last state of that man is worse than the first."**

THE PRE-ADAMIC RACE:

Unclean spirits don't like to be cast out, so if they have an opportunity to re-enter or re-attach, they will. Unclean spirits are demons. Demons are not fallen angels like many people think they are. Demons are the disembodied spirits of the Pre-Adamic Race of beings that were here before Adam and Eve. These people were Lucifer's people. Fallen angels are chained in hell until the Great White Throne Judgment. The Word of God clearly shows us that:

2 Peter 2:4 "For if God spared not the angels that sinned, but cast them down to hell, and delivered them into chains of darkness, to be reserved unto judgment."

Jude 6 **"And the angels which kept not their first estate, but left their own habitation, he hath reserved in everlasting chains under darkness**

unto the judgment of the great day."

Let's now take a look at Genesis 1 to lay the Scriptural foundation for the Pre-Adamic Race. Let's start off with verse 1:

Genesis 1:1 **"In the beginning God created the heaven and the earth."**

God is perfect and everything He creates is created in perfection. Verse 1 refers to the very beginning. Let's look now at verse 2:

Genesis 1:2 **"And the earth was without form, and void; and darkness was upon the face of the deep. And the Spirit of God moved upon the face of the waters."**

So what happened between verse 1 and verse 2 ? Well, in the beginning God created everything in perfection. Sometime later, we don't know, it could be millions, even billions of years, the earth was now without form and was void. This means it was waste and empty. Well, we know God doesn't create things waste and empty, so how did it become this way? It became that way because of sin. The sin of Lucifer and his people.

***Isaiah 45:18* "For thus saith the Lord that created the heavens; God himself that formed the earth and made it; he hath established it, he created it not in vain, he formed it to be inhabited: I am the Lord; and there is none else."**

In Genesis chapter one verse two, we see the Spirit of God moving upon the waters, so we see the existence of the earth and of the water, and darkness before the first day of the Adamic creation. God created the earth to be inhabited, and we see right in the Word that it was inhabited before verse 2 in Genesis chapter 1 - before the six days of the time of Adam and

Eve, which started in the third verse of Genesis. We see in verse 2 of Genesis 1 that after God's original creation of the earth and heaven, that the earth was flooded with water. There was no light, only darkness. Everything was destroyed. In order for this to happen, there had to have been something there to start with. The Pre-Adamic race. Let's continue on with our Scriptural foundation by looking at Jeremiah chapter 4:

Jeremiah 4:23-28 **"I beheld the earth, and lo, it was without form, and void; and the heavens, and they had no light. I beheld the mountains, and lo, they trembled, and all the hills moved lightly. I beheld and lo, there was no man, and all the birds of the heavens were fled. I beheld, and lo, the fruitful place was a wilderness, and all the cities thereof were broken down at the presence of the Lord, and by his fierce anger. For thus hath the Lord said, The**

whole land shall be desolate; yet will I not make a full end. For this shall the earth mourn, and the heavens above be black: because I have spoken it, I have purposed it, and will not repent, neither will I turn back from it."

When the Word says "in the beginning", it's not referring to the 6 days of creation which is about 6,000 years or so ago. The first verse in Genesis 1 means an un-named date in the past. Like I said, we don't know when it was. God commanded His creation to replenish the earth - meaning to fill it again. Well, that means that this earth had to have been filled prior to Adam's time.

Genesis 1:28 **"And God blessed them, and God said unto them, Be fruitful, and multiply, and replenish the earth, and subdue it: and have dominion over the fish of the sea, and over the fowl of the air, and** over every living thing that moveth upon the earth."

We also see in Genesis chapter 9 that God gave this same command to Noah just after the second flood upon the earth.

Genesis 9:1 "And God blessed Noah and his sons, and said unto them, Be fruitful, and multiply, and replenish the earth."

A pre-adamic race just makes sense. It also explains the dinosaurs. In fact, we see in the book of Job, the mention of the behemoth. Let's read:

Job 40:15-24 "Behold now behemoth, which I made with thee; he eateth grass as an ox. Lo now, his strength is in his loins, and his force is in the navel of his belly. He moveth his tail like a cedar: the sinews of his stones are wrapped together. His bones are as strong pieces of brass; his bones are like bars of iron. He is the chief of the ways of God: he that made him can make his sword to approach unto him. Surely the mountains bring him forth food, where all the beasts of the field play. He lieth under the shady trees, in the covert of the reed, and fens. The shady trees cover him with their shadow; the willows of the brook compass him about. Behold, he drinketh up a river, and hasteth not: he trusteth that he can draw up Jordan into his mouth. He taketh it with his eyes: his nose pierceth through snares."

Lucifer, who became Satan, the devil, had already ruled the earth, and had already become a fallen creature before the time of Adam and Eve. This is proof that Adam's Race was not the first ones on the earth. When Satan came into the Garden of Eden as the serpent, he had already fallen. (See **Genesis 3:1, 2 Corinthians 11:3**).

Lucifer made an invasion of heaven from the earth in hopes of defeating Almighty God and take His kingdom from Him. However, his plans went astray, and he was defeated and his people were cursed. Lucifer was trying to be God, and it didn't work. There is only one God, and no other. Prior to this, Lucifer had a kingdom of people to rule over on this earth. He was the organizer of the worship, on the holy mountain of God. All of this occurred before Adam and Eve's time on earth. Let's look now at Isaiah chapter 14 where we see the record of Lucifer's fall:

Isaiah 14:12-20 **"How art thou fallen from heaven, O Lucifer, son of the morning! How art thou cut down to the ground, which didst weaken the nations! For thou hast said in thine heart, I will ascend into heaven, I will exalt my throne above the stars of God; I will sit also upon the mount of the congregation, in the** sides of the north: I will ascend above the heights of the clouds; I will be like the Most High. Yet thou shalt be brought down to hell, to the sides of the pit. They that see thee shall narrowly look upon thee, and consider thee, saying, Is this the man that made the earth to tremble, that did shake kingdoms; That made the world as a wilderness, and destroyed the cities thereof; that opened not the house of his prisoners? All the kings of the nations, even all of them lie in glory, every one in his own house. But thou art cast down out of thy grave like an abominable branch, and as the raiment of those that are slain, thrust through with a sword, that go down to the stones of the pit; as a carcase trodden under feet. Thou shalt not be joined with them in burial, because thou hast destroyed thy land, and slain thy people: the seed of evildoers shall never be renowned."

The Pre-Adamic Race of beings were slain, and they remain name-less because of their evil. That's why we refer to them as the pre-adamic race, or the pre-adamites. Ezekiel chapter 28 gives us a detailed description of Lucifer before his fall. Let's take a look:

Ezekiel 28:11-19 **"Moreover the Word of the Lord came unto me, saying, son of man take up a lamentation upon the king of Tyrus, and say unto him, Thus saith the Lord God; thou sealest up the sum full of wisdom, and perfect in beauty. Thou hast been in Eden, the garden of God; every precious stone was thy covering; the sardius, topaz, and the diamond, the beryl, the onyx, and the jasper, the sapphire, the emerald, and the carbuncle, and gold: the workmanship of thy tabrets and of thy pipes was prepared in thee in the day that thou was created. Thou art the anointed** cherub that cover-eth; and I have set thee so: thou wast upon the holy mountain of God; thou hast walked up and down in the midst of the stones of fire. Thou wast perfect in thy ways from the day that thou wast created, till iniquity was found in thee. By the multitude of thy merchandise they have filled the midst of thee with violence, and thou hast sinned: therefore I will cast thee as profane out of the mountain of God; and I will destroy thee, O covering cherub, from the midst of the stones of fire. Thine heart was lifted up because of thy beauty, thou hast corrupted thy wisdom by reason of thy brightness: I will cast thee to the ground, I will lay thee before kings, that they may behold thee. Thou hast defiled thy sanctuaries by the multitude of thine iniquities, by the iniquity of thy traffick; therefore will I bring forth a fire from the midst of thee, it shall devour thee, and I will bring thee to

ashes upon the earth in the sight of all them that behold thee. All they that know thee among the people shall be astonished at thee: thou shalt be a terror, and never shalt thou be any more."

Because of Lucifer's pride, which was the first sin, he was cast down. Since that time he has concocted an agenda to trip up anyone who would follow God and have dominion. First he started on Adam and Eve in the Garden of Eden, and it continues now in the present day. Whether you believe or not about the Pre-Adamic race, it's not a salvation requirement, but I believe it's important to know about this, especially for those of us who want to be anointed for battle. Because in order to successfully cast out demons and wage successful spiritual warfare, we need to have the facts straight. We need to know how our enemy works so we can overcome him at every turn. Jesus Himself was in Heaven at this time, and He witnessed the fall of Lucifer. This of course happened before Jesus came to earth as a flesh and blood person. Nevertheless, Jesus has always existed, and He got to see the old serpent Lucifer cast down out of heaven by God the Father. Look at Luke chapter 10:

***Luke 10:18* "And He said unto them, I beheld Satan as lightning fall from heaven."**

Satan is still a defeated foe. Make no mistake about that. But he still tries every way he can to trip up believers. He knows his time is short, so whatever he can do to seduce a person, he will try it. One of the biggest ways is false doctrine. Let's now continue our studies by looking at a few of the sacred cows filling the church today, starting with "Once Saved, Always Saved".

CONDITIONAL SECURITY OF THE BELIEVER:

Jesus our Lord preached cause and effect. In many Churches and Ministries, believers are being told that all they have to do is say a simple little prayer and they are completely saved, and no matter that they do, they will go to heaven. This false doctrine known as Once Saved, Always Saved - is a lie from the very pit of hell. It's a doctrine of demons, and the devil is having a heyday with it. People are deceived to think that all they do is utter a prayer, then live like the devil the rest of their life never even acknowledging God. They think they are going to float on a glory cloud strumming a harp singing Alleluia. The promoters of OSAS, also known as Eternal security, are really in actuality, giving believers a license to sin. They think that because they are saved by grace, they can go out and do as they please, because after all, "I'm saved". One man even told me that a person who gets saved can even go out and commit the vilest of sins such as murder, and still go to heaven - without repenting and getting right with God. What a lie! What utter blasphemy!

***Jude 4* "For there are certain men crept in unawares, who were before of old ordained to this condemnation, ungodly men, turning the grace of our God into lasciviousness, and denying the only Lord God, and our Lord Jesus Christ."**

These "once saved, always saved" people usually only use three or four verses to "prove" their position, but they take the Scriptures out of context, and won't listen to the truth. As we see in this passage from Jude, there are people who use grace as a license to sin and live like the world does. These charlatans have crept in unaware, meaning that they have infiltrated the churches, and many don't even see it. These people turn the grace of God into "lasciviousness". Lasciviousness means "unrestraint". These types walk in the lust of the flesh, and encourage others to do so as well. We must not be deceived by these people. We must walk in the full measure of the Truth. Now, let's examine some of the verses the OSAS crowd like to use to defend their position:

***John 10:27-29* "My sheep hear my voice, and I know them, and they follow me: And I give unto them eternal life; and they shall never perish, neither shall any man pluck them out of my hand. My Father which gave them me, is greater than all, and no man is able to pluck them out of my Father's hand."**

While it is true that no man can pluck you out of God's hand, a person does have free will, and can leave anytime they choose. God won't override your free will. Even the devil can't pluck you out of God's hand. If you don't submit to God, your disobedience let's the devil in to influence you. However, in the end, it's your own free will choice to either walk with God fully, or not. There is eternal security - once you get to heaven, but as long as you are walking this earth, final salvation is conditional upon obedience to Christ. This is not to say that God is going to get us on a technicality. Far from it. But we need to use wisdom to know that we cannot go out and commit willful sin and think God winks at that. He doesn't. He is a holy and righteous God, and desires us to be holy also. Let's look at first Peter 1:

1 Peter 1:13-16 **"Wherefore gird up the lions of your mind, be sober, and hope to the end for the grace that is to be brought unto you at the revelation of Jesus Christ. As obedient children, not fashioning yourselves according to the former**

lusts in your ignorance: But as He which hath called you is holy, so be ye holy in all manner of conversation; Because it is written, Be ye holy; for I am holy."

1 John 2:6 **"He that saith he abideth in him ought himself also so to walk, even as he walked."**

The next verse that is commonly used by the eternal security - OSAS promoters, is from Romans chapter 8:

Romans 8:38-39 **"For I am persuaded that neither death, nor life, nor angels, nor principalities, nor powers, nor things present, nor things to come, nor height, nor depth, nor any other creature, shall be able to separate us from the love of God, which is in Christ Jesus our Lord."**

Though the false teachers would say otherwise, this passage is not talking about salvation. It's talking about the love of God, and the persecution we endure because of our stand for Him. Nothing will ever separate God's love for us. Even if you choose to go to the lake of fire by your own disobedience, God still loves you. Two things are missing from this passage - yourself, and the past. You can choose to walk away from God and the love He has for you. You can also let the past prevent you from moving forward with the Lord. Again, it's a free will choice everyone has to make. Now let's take a look at some of the Scriptures that the OSAS crowd like to side-step. The reason they do - is because they don't have ears to hear the truth, only what their itching ears want to hear.

2 Peter 2:20-22 **"For if after they have escaped the pollutions of the world through the knowledge of the Lord and Savior Jesus Christ, they are again entangled therein, and overcome, the latter end is worse**

with them than the beginning. For it had been better for them not to have known the way of righteousness, than after they have known it, to turn from the holy commandment delivered unto them. But it is happened unto them according to the true proverb, The dog is turned to his own vomit again; and the sow that was washed to her wallowing in the mire."

This Scripture clearly shows us that there are those who are saved that turn away from the Lord, and go back to their old lifestyles. It's so very plain in the Word, yet so many don't see. Others just don't WANT to see it. The real truth of the matter is that they love their sin. They have an evil heart of unbelief, causing them to depart from faith in God.

Hebrews 3:12 **"Take heed, brethren, lest there be in any of you an evil heart of unbelief, in departing from**

the living God."

This verse clearly shows that there are brethren - meaning believers, who do depart from their faith in God. It's right there, plain in the Word of God. I didn't make it up. People, we need to take heed to what the Word says. Don't think you can use grace for an occasion to sin. Grace is God's unmerited favor, not a license to sin. Let's read now in first Corinthians 15 as we continue our study:

1 Corinthians 15:1-2 **"Moreover, brethren, I declare unto you the Gospel which I preached unto you, Which also ye have received, and wherein ye stand; By which also ye are saved, If ye keep in memory what I preached unto you, unless ye have believed in vain."**

Notice the "if" in this verse. There's the cause and effect again. Every believer should go and underline, circle, or highlight the word "if" in their Bibles. Many people believe in vain, and don't truly follow Christ. These follow after their own lusts. We must not think that we can tempt God and just live any old way and get a full inheritance. It doesn't work that way. We are commanded to be obedient, and to overcome. When we do, we have a place with Jesus right there in His throne.

***Revelation 3:21-22* "To him that overcometh will I grant to sit with me in my throne, even as I also overcame, and am set down with my Father in his throne. He that hath an ear, let him hear what the Spirit saith unto the churches."**

Another Scripture that the OSAS promoters like to use to say that we are eternally secure on this earth no matter what, is the very well known verse - John 3:16. Let's read this verse:

John 3:16 **"For God so loved the world, that he gave his only begotten Son, that whosoever believeth in Him should not perish, but have everlasting life."**

Yes, absolutely we are going to have everlasting life. But we need to understand the full meaning of what Jesus is saying in this verse. Jesus said that those who believeth in Him should not perish. Believing is not just a one time occurrence. You don't just believe once and then forget about Him. To truly believe is to believe every single second that you live and breathe. True believers keep on believing right up until that last trump sounds, and we are raptured out of here. For someone to say that you believe in Christ once after saying a prayer, and then go about with your life not ever even acknowledging God, or living for Him, is to give someone a false perception of God. Our wonderful Lord Jesus shed His precious blood on the Cross for the sins of the whole world. He gave His life for us so that we could be free. How dare some man or woman stand behind a pulpit or behind a webcam and declare such nonsense like "once saved, always saved". How dare these people. Jesus Christ ultimate sacrifice is not to be taken for granted. But that is what is happening with these embracers of OSAS. They are literally spitting upon what our Lord did for us on the Cross. What blasphemy! What a heinous crime against the God Who has given us life. Let's look now at the book of John, chapter 15, where Jesus speaks of those who abide in Him, and those who don't:

John 15:1-8 **"I am the true vine, and My Father is the husbandman. Every branch in me that beareth not fruit he taketh away: and every branch that beareth fruit, he purgeth it, that it may bring forth more fruit. Now ye are clean**

through the word which I have spoken unto you. Abide in Me, and I in you. As the branch cannot bear fruit of itself, except it abide in the vine; no more can ye, except ye abide in me. I am the vine, ye are the branches: He that abideth in me, and I in him, the same bringeth forth much fruit: for without me ye can do nothing. If a man abide not in Me, he is cast forth as a branch, and is withered; and men gather them, and cast them into the fire, and they are burned. If ye abide in Me, and my words abide in you, ye shall ask what ye will, and it shall be done unto you. Herein is my Father glorified, that ye bear much fruit; so shall ye be my disciples."

Yet again, we see cause and effect in action in this passage. Jesus said that if a man does not abide in Him, then that man is a withered branch who is cast into the fire and burned. Jesus went on to tell us that God the Father is

glorified when His people are fruit bearers. These are the very ones that He considers to be His true disciples - the sons of obedience.
Now let's examine a few more Scriptures that prove that "once saved, always saved" is a false doctrine.
God's Word is the Final Authority, and is with what we measure everything.

***Hebrews 6:4-6* "For it is impossible for those who were once enlightened and have tasted of the heavenly gift, and were made partakers of the Holy Ghost, And have tasted the good word of God, and the powers of the world to come, If they shall fall away, to renew them again unto repentance; seeing they crucify to themselves the Son of God afresh, and put Him to an open shame."**

This verse from Hebrews 6 is talking about those people who were believers at one point, then fell away because of committing an eternal sin such as blasphemy against the Holy Spirit - which is the one unpardonable sin. (See **Mark 3:28-30**). Now, this is not to say that a person can never be forgiven of any other sin and return to the Lord. Absolutely they can come back to Him. However, those people who commit the unpardonable sin of blasphemy against the Holy Spirit cannot be renewed unto repentance. This, as everything else we have looked at, wipes out "once saved, always saved".

Ezekiel 18:24,26,32 **"But when the righteous turneth away from his righteousness, and commiteth iniquity, and doeth according to all the abominations that the wicked man doeth, shall he live? All his righteousness that he hath done shall not be mentioned: in his trespass that he hath trespassed, and in his sin that he hath sinned, in them shall he die."**

Verse 26 "When a righteous man turneth away from his righteousness, and committeth iniquity, and dieth in them, for his iniquity that he hath done shall he die."

Verse 32 "For I have no pleasure in the death of him that dieth, saith the Lord God: Wherefore turn yourselves, and live ye."

We clearly see, yet again, that there are those who are righteous in the Lord, who turn away from Him, and commit sin without repentance. God doesn't want any to die and go to hell. God desires that all would turn from their sins and truly follow Him. Sadly, many fall away, and go back to the world and it's lust. The love of the world has blinded the eyes of so many, and has caused them to abandon their First Love.

2 Peter 3:9 "The Lord is not slack

concerning his promise, as some men count slackness; but is longsuffering to us-ward, not willing that any should perish, but that all should come to repentance."

1 John 1:9 "If we confess our sins, He is faithful and just to forgive us our sins, and to cleanse us from all unrighteousness."

1 John 2:15-17 "Love not the world, neither the things that are in the world. If any man love the world, the love of the Father is not in him. For all that is in the world, the lust of the flesh, and the lust of the eyes, and the pride of life, is not of the Father, but is of the world. And the world passeth away, and the lust thereof: but he that doeth the will of God abideth for ever."

We also see in The Word, that there are those whose names are removed from The Book of Life. Well, to be removed from it means they had to have been there to start with! Makes sense, doesn't it? We see clear reference from both Old and New Testaments. Let's take a look:

Exodus 32:32-33 **"Yet now, if thou wilt forgive their sin -; and if not, blot me, I pray thee out of thy book which thou hast written. And the Lord said unto Moses, Whosoever hath sinned against me, him will I blot out of my book."**

Psalms 69:28 **"Let them be blotted out of the book of the living, and not be written with the righteous."**

Revelation 3:5 **"He that overcometh the same shall be clothed in white raiment; and I will not blot out his name out of the book of life, but I will confess his name before my Father, and before His angels."**

We can clearly see from these verses

that those who sin against God and remain unrepentant will be blotted out of The Book of Life. This is very serious business, church. We cannot afford to take any of this lightly. Don't be sidelined by false teachers that just want to tell you that you can live any old way you want to, and you're ok. The kingdom doesn't work that way. Yes - we will make mistakes and miss it sometimes. We are still in a flesh and bone body. However, that does not mean that we can go on willfully sinning - living like the devil, and think that God will reward that. Think again. Just because we are under grace in this New Covenant does not mean that we are to live like the world. As a follower of Jesus Christ, we are to live and move and have our being in Him. (See **Acts 17:28**). Our lives and character are to be molded after Him. Just about every person that I have talked to who believes OSAS, has a filthy mouth. That right there shows the "fruit" of "once saved, always saved". So called Christians using profanity, and not caring one bit. This is another reason that OSAS is so dangerous and defiling. People can offend as they please because after all, "they are saved by grace and eternally secure". What foolish nonsense! Look what the Word of God says about those who are perverse in their ways:

Proverbs 28:18 **"Whoso walketh uprightly shall be saved: but he that is perverse in his ways shall fall at once."**

The eternal life that Jesus promised us is conditional upon us remaining IN Christ, and living for Him. So when fellowship is lost, relationship means nothing at all. When we get to heaven we are going to be having constant fellowship with God. So is a person thinks that they can be out of fellowship with God here on this earth, why then would God want to take them to heaven to have fellowship with them there? It makes absolutely no sense, right? True fellowship, and true relationship is what our God is looking for in and with His children. The church has been so seduced by doctrines of demons (such as OSAS), that they are departing from the true faith. (See 1 Timothy 4:1-5). These people have gotten the wrong idea that they can believe on Jesus without obeying Him at all. Let's look now at the book of John, chapter 3:

***John 3:36* "He that believeth on the Son hath everlasting life: and he that believeth not the Son shall not see life; but the wrath of God abideth on him."**

The words "believeth not" from this passage of Scripture in John 3 is the Greek word "apeitheo" which means "not believe", "disobedient", "obey not", & "unbelieving". This shows us that being disobedient is also unbelief. Now let's read this very same verse in

The New American Standard Bible:

John 3:36 "He who believes in the Son has eternal life; but he who does not obey the Son shall not see life, but the wrath of God abides on him."
                    (NASB)

Let's now look at the book of Hebrews for yet another Scripture that shows us the importance of obedience:

Hebrews 5:8-9 "Though he were a Son, yet learned he obedience by the things which he suffered; And being made perfect, he became the author of eternal salvation unto all them that obey Him."

Jesus was obedient, and He has become the Author of eternal salvation to all them that OBEY HIM. Again, if you don't obey Him, it shows that you are in unbelief, and have departed from the faith. Eternal salvation is freely available to anyone who will obey God and follow Him. And the Bible also makes it very clear that not everyone who mouths " Lord, Lord", shall enter into His kingdom. There are conditions upon entering. Those who use His Name in vain, and for greedy gain will not go unpunished. And yes, even anointed men and women can get off into the flesh. People will have to give an account of what happens "behind the scenes". Let's read in Matthew chapter 7:

Matthew 7:21-27 **"Not every one that saith unto me, Lord, Lord, shall enter into the kingdom of heaven; but he that doeth the will of my Father which is in heaven. Many will say to me in that day, Lord, Lord, have we not prophesied in thy name? and in thy name have cast out devils? And in thy name done many wonderful works? And then will I profess unto them, I never knew you: depart from me, ye that** work iniquity. Therefore whosoever heareth these sayings of mine, and doeth them, I will liken him unto a wise man, which built his house upon a rock: And the rain descended, and the floods came, and the winds blew, and beat upon that house; and it fell not: for it was founded upon a rock. And every one that heareth these sayings of mine, and doeth them not, shall be likened unto a foolish man, which built his house upon the sand: And the rain descended, and the floods came, and the winds blew, and beat upon that house, and it fell: and great was the fall of it."**

Once saved, always saved? - I don't think so!

THE CURSE OF THE LAW:

The next thing that I would like to look at is the Covenant that we have with

God. As New Covenant believers, we have been redeemed from the curse of the Law - the old Mosaic Law and all it's curses, and all the rituals attached to it. Jesus Christ paid for everything on the Cross. The curse of poverty, sickness and disease, and the handwriting of ordinances was all nailed to the Cross.

Galatians 3:10-14, 23-29 **"For as many as are of the works of the law are under the curse: for it is written, Cursed is every one that continueth not in all things which are written in the book of the law to do them. But that no man is justified by the law in the sight of God, it is evident: for the just shall live by faith. And the law is not of faith; but the man that doeth them shall live in them. Christ hath redeemed us from the curse of the law, being made a curse for us: for it is written, Cursed is every one that hangeth on a tree: That the blessing of Abraham might come on** the Gentiles through Jesus Christ; that we might receive the promise of the Spirit through faith."

Verses 23-29 "But before faith came, we were kept under the law, shut up unto the faith which should afterwards be revealed. Wherefore the law was our schoolmaster to bring us unto Christ, that we might be justified by faith. But after that faith is come, we are no longer under a schoolmaster. For ye are all the children of God by faith in Christ Jesus. For as many of you as have been baptized into Christ have put on Christ. There is neither Jew nor Greek, there is neither bond nor free, there is neither male nor female: for ye are all one in Christ Jesus. And if ye be Christ's, then are ye Abraham's seed, and heirs according to the promise."

Colossians 2:14-15 "Blotting out the handwriting of ordinances that was

against us, which was contrary to us, and took it out of the way, nailing it to His cross; And having spoiled principalities and powers, He made a shew of them openly, triumphing over them in it."

We as blood-bought believers are no longer under the old Mosaic Law. We are under grace by faith in Jesus Christ, and are led by the Holy Spirit. To the unbeliever - the Law brings the knowledge of their sin, but after you accept Jesus as your Savior, and are born again of the Holy Spirit, you are no longer subject to the letter of the Law. Jesus Christ nailed it to His Cross on Calvary.

Romans 3:20 **"Therefore by the deeds of the law there shall no flesh be justified in his sight: for by the law is the knowledge of sin."**

The Mosaic Law was given to the Jews as a punishment for their sin and idolatry. It wasn't meant as a good thing. However, there are believers who see no problem going back under the old Law. They don't realize that they are bringing the curse back upon them, and are separating themselves from faith in the Lord Jesus Christ.

Romans 7:4,6 **"Wherefore, my brethren, ye also are become dead to the law by the body of Christ; that ye should be married to another, even to him who is raised from the dead, that we should bring forth fruit unto God."**

Verse 6 **"But now we are delivered from the law, that being dead wherein we were held, that we should serve in newness of Spirit, and not in the oldness of the letter."**

2 Corinthians 3:5-6 **"Not that we are sufficient of ourselves to think any thing as of ourselves; but our sufficiency is of God; Who also hath**

made us able ministers of the new testament; not of the letter, but of the Spirit: for the letter killeth, but the Spirit giveth life."

When someone who is a Christian goes back to the old Law, he is taking himself out of God's covering, which is a faith covering. The Promise is eternal, and it is through faith and righteousness of Christ, not through the Law.

Romans 4:13-14 **"For the promise that he should be the heir of the world, was not to Abraham or to his seed, through the law, but through the righteousness of faith. For if they which are of the law be heirs, faith is made void, and the promise made of none effect."**

Those who take themselves out of God's covering by embracing the old Law, now must obey all 613 laws, which is impossible. That's the reason for Jesus coming to redeem us. No one can keep 613 laws, that's one of the reasons we need redemption and faith in Christ. We put our faith and trust in Christ Jesus, not in the dead Law. Apparently, these people who are subject to the old ordinances and all the trappings of the Mosaic Law don't think Christ's blood was enough. In fact - His blood is more than enough. It is all sufficient. Jesus Christ redeemed us from the curse and letter of the Law, so why would someone want to go back under it? Jewish traditions - such as the feasts and the festivals, and related rituals are not something that a blood-bought, redeemed believer should be involved in. All this does is put you back under the curse, Right back where the devil wants you. You don't need to follow Old Testament dietary laws, abstaining from pork and such. In the New Covenant, God says all food is good to eat. Just pray over it, and bless it in Jesus Name. It is sanctified by prayer and The Word.

(See **1 Timothy 4:1-5**). When the people of the days of the Mosaic Law sinned, they had to go around wearing their sin and shame as a garment. This was to remind them of their sin and disobedience to the commandments.

Numbers 15:37-41 **"And the Lord spake unto Moses, saying, Speak unto the children of Israel, and bid them that they make them fringes in the borders of their garments throughout their generations, and that they put upon the fringe of the borders a ribband of blue: And it shall be unto you for a fringe, that ye may look upon it, and remember all the commandments of the Lord, and do them; and that ye seek not after your own heart and your own eyes, after which ye use to go a whoring: That ye may remember, and do all my commandments, and be holy unto your God. I am the Lord your God, which brought you out of the land of Egypt, to be your**

God: I am the Lord your God."

Well, under the New Covenant, under faith in Jesus Christ, we have a Mighty Savior and Lord Who forgives us of our sins when we repent, and cleanses us from all unrighteousness, and casts our sins into the depths of the sea. (See **1 John 1:9, Hebrews 8:12, Micah 7:18-19**). Christ Jesus wipes the slate clean and doesn't require us to wear a prayer shawl with the requirements of the Old Law on it. Through the death, burial, resurrection, and Holy Spirit, we are redeemed from the curse of the Law. The promise is eternal, but the letter is dead.

Galatians 5:1, 4-5, 9, 18 **"Stand fast therefore in the liberty wherewith Christ hath made us free, and be not entangled again with the yoke of bondage."**

Verses 4-5 **"Christ is become of no effect unto you, whosoever of you** are justified by the law; ye are fallen from grace. For we through the Spirit wait for the hope of righteousness by faith."

Verse 9 "A little leaven leaveneth the whole lump."

Verse 18 "But if ye be led of the Spirit, ye are not under the law."

We clearly see that those who are trying to be justified by the old Law, separate themselves from Christ, and have fallen from grace. Even a little of the Law being embraced by a believer ruins the whole. We must trust only in Jesus Christ and His shed blood, and walk and live our lives by faith, and by the leading of the Holy Spirit. The body of Christ is not to be defiled, but that is what is taking place when professing Christians embrace the Law and think it's ok. Those who truly want to walk with Christ, and have the anointing for battle upon their lives, are going to have to keep the Mosaic Law where it belongs - nailed to the Cross of Calvary. We have a New, and better Covenant through Jesus Christ and His ultimate Sacrifice. Glory be to God!

Hebrews 7:22 **"By so much was Jesus made a surety of a better testament."**

Hebrews 8:6-8, 13 **"But now hath he obtained a more excellent ministry, by how much also he is the mediator of a better covenant, which was established upon better promises. For if that first covenant had been faultless, then should no place have been sought for the second. For finding fault with them, he saith, Behold, the days come saith the Lord, when I will make a new covenant with the house of Israel and with the house of Judah...."**

Verse 13 **"In that he saith a new**

covenant, he hath made the first old. Now that which decayeth and waxeth old is ready to vanish away."

Galatians 3:19 **"Wherefore then serveth the law? It was added because of transgressions, till the Seed should come to whom the promise was made; and it was ordained by angels in the hand of a mediator."**

In the Old Covenant, under the Law, sin and disobedience brought the curse upon people's lives. In the New Covenant, which we are in, we have much better promises, and we have the blessings of God poured out upon us. A covenant is a contract, an agreement that is made between two parties, and is sealed by their blood being shed, and this means that the covenant cannot ever be broken. Praise God we have a blood Covenant through Jesus Christ. Jesus completely fulfilled all the terms of the Old Covenant, and then He gave His life for the sins of the world on the Cross.

John 3:16 **"For God so loved the world, that he gave his only begotten Son, that whosoever believeth in him should not perish, but have everlasting life."**

Jesus said **"It is finished." (John 19:30**). His Sacrifice on the Cross was finished. He did the very will of the Father, and He bore all the sins, all the sicknesses, all the diseases, and all the poverties and oppression of this world. In the Old Covenant, we had the shedding of man's blood through circumcision. In the New Covenant, we have the shedding of Jesus' blood on the Cross. The punishment (curse) of the old Law included poverty, sickness, and also spiritual death. All three of these are curses of the Law, and if a believer goes back to the old Law, he brings all three of these horrible things right back upon himself. Going back to the Law puts the believer back in bondage. We saw earlier in Galatians 5 that we are to stand in the liberty of Christ. We are not to be entangled with bondage. Bondage is from the devil, and we as believers have authority over the devil. We are not justified by the Law, but by faith in Christ Jesus. Look at these verses from Galatians chapter 2:

Galatians 2:16, 21 **"Knowing that a man is not justified by the works of the law, but by the faith of Jesus Christ, even we have believed in Jesus Christ, that we might be justified by the faith of Christ, and not by the works of the law: for by the works of the law shall no flesh be justified."**

Verse 21 **"I do not frustrate the grace of God: for if righteousness come by the law, then Christ is dead in vain."**

We are to follow Christ and His commandments, and walk in our authority. We are to embrace the newness of life - the New Covenant, not the dead Law that was nailed to the Cross. Don't be deceived by the devil or anyone who tries to bring you back under the curse. Start embracing the Covenant that God has for you - His New Covenant that is established upon much better promises. Tithing pre-dated the Law, and is a part of the Promise. It involves being obedient unto God, and trusting Him in all aspects of your life. Tithing and giving of offerings into good ground is essential if we want to reap God's supernatural harvest. When we give above the tithe, the Word says that our seed sown will be multiplied and increased.

Galatians 3:16-18 **"Now to Abraham and his seed were the promises made. He saith not, And to seeds, as of many; but as of one, And to thy**

Seed, which is Christ. And this I say, that the covenant, that was confirmed before of God in Christ, the law, which was four hundred and thirty years after, cannot disannul, that it should make the promise of none effect. For if the inheritance be of the law, it is no more of promise: but God gave it to Abraham by promise."

Malachi 3:10-12 "Bring ye all the tithes into the storehouse, that there may be meat in mine house, and prove me now herewith, saith the Lord of hosts, if I will not open you the windows of heaven, and pour you out a blessing, that there shall not be room enough to receive it. And I will rebuke the devourer for your sakes, and he shall not destroy the fruits of your ground; neither shall your vine cast her fruit before the time in the field, saith the Lord of hosts. And all nations shall call you blessed: for ye shall be a delightsome land, saith the Lord of hosts."

2 Corinthians 9:6-11 "But this I say, he which soweth sparingly shall reap also sparingly; and he which soweth bountifully shall reap also bountifully. Every man according as he purposeth in his heart, so let him give; not grudgingly, or of necessity: for God loveth a cheerful giver. And God is able to make all grace abound toward you; that ye, always having all sufficiency in all things, may abound to every good work: (As it is written, he hath dispersed abroad; he hath given to the poor: his righteousness remaineth for ever. Now he that ministereth seed to the sower both minister bread for your food, and multiply your seed sown, and increase the fruits of your righteousness;) Being enriched in every thing to all bountifulness, which causeth through us thanksgiving to God."

And when you tithe and sow your seed, don't just put it anywhere. You need to sow it in good ground. You need to sow your seed and your tithe into God's storehouses - where the full-Gospel is being preached without compromise.

OUR IDENTITY IN CHRIST:

The next thing I want to focus on is our identity in Christ. In many places in the Bible we see the phrase "in Christ". But I truly wonder if many Christians understand what being in Christ really means. As blood bought and baptized in the Holy Spirit believers, our identity is in Jesus Christ. In Christ we have an eternal inheritance that awaits us, but if we lose sight of our identity, the inheritance can be forfeited. Those believers who lose their identity in Christ probably do so because they don't really know what their identity is in the first place. Let's read in second Corinthians to start off:

***2 Corinthians 5:17, 21* "Therefore if any man be in Christ, he is a new creature: Old things are passed away; behold, all things are become new."**

***Verse 21* "For he hath made him to be sin for us, who knew no sin, that we might be made the righteousness of God in him."**

In Christ Jesus, we are new creatures, the old things have passed away, and we now have newness of life in Him. In Christ we have been made righteous through His shed blood. The Word of God says that we are complete in Him. (See **Colossians 2:10**). Christians everywhere need to start boldly proclaiming who God says we are, not what man says.

2 Corinthians 2:14-15 "Now thanks

be unto God, which always causeth us to triumph in Christ, and maketh manifest the savour of his knowledge by us in every place. For we are unto God a sweet savour of Christ in them that are saved, and in them that perish."

In Christ, we are overcomers who always triumph. Just think about it. Your life would drastically change if you would truly grasp who you are in Christ. The Word says that we have been raised with Christ Jesus and are seated together with Him in heavenly places. We are identified with Christ in every aspect. Look at what it says in the book of Ephesians:

Ephesians 2:4-7, 10, 13 **"But God who is rich in mercy, for his great love wherewith he loves us, even when we were dead in sins, hath quickened us together with Christ (by grace ye are saved); And hath raised us up together and made us** sit together in heavenly places in Christ Jesus: That in the ages to come he might shew the exceeding riches of his grace in his kindness toward us through Christ Jesus."

Verse 10 "For we are his workmanship, created in Christ Jesus unto good works, which God hath before ordained that we should walk in them."

Verse 13 "But now in Christ Jesus, ye who sometimes were far off are made nigh by the blood of Christ."

The key to receiving from God, and walking in the newness of life, and having His power in your life, is finding your place IN CHRIST. This will require that your thinking and your speaking have a change. In Christ Jesus we are made righteous, we are triumphant, victorious, and blessed beyond measure. In Christ, we are redeemed by His blood, and redeemed from the curse of the Law, and the curse of sin. In Christ we have a new heritage, and a new identity. Redemption is an accomplished fact in Christ. Praise God!

***1 Timothy 2:5-6* "For there is one God, and one Mediator between God and men, the Man Christ Jesus; Who gave himself a ransom for all, to be testified in due time."**

God paid the full price for us some 2,000 years ago - IN CHRIST. Don't think for one minute that Christianity ever begins with something we do or have done. Christianity began with something that has already been done for us IN CHRIST. Everything that we need is supplied for us in Christ. It was all done and paid for in His death, burial, and resurrection. He did it for us - on our behalf. We can rejoice in the finished work of the Cross. Jesus said **"It is finished"**.

John 19:30 "When Jesus therefore had received the vinegar, he said, It is finished: and he bowed his head, and gave up the ghost."

1 Corinthians 15:3-4 "For I delivered unto you first of all that which I also received, how that Christ died for our sins according to the scriptures; And that he was buried, and that he rose again the third day according to the scriptures."

In Christ, we have been delivered from the powers of darkness, and have been made partakers of God's divine inheritance. And this inheritance contains everything we will ever need.

Colossians 1:12-14 "Giving thanks unto the Father, which hath made us meet to be partakers of the inheritance of the saints in light: Who hath delivered us from the power of darkness, and hath translated us into the kingdom of his dear Son: In whom we have redemption through his blood, even the forgiveness of sins."

Ephesians 1:3 "Blessed be the God and Father of our Lord Jesus Christ, who hath blessed us with all spiritual blessings in heavenly places in Christ."

Every spiritual blessing there is, is made available to us in Christ, and will never change. God is a good God, and He always desires to bless and prosper His children. That's the kind of God we serve!

James 1:17 "Every good gift and every perfect gift is from above, and cometh down from the Father of lights, with whom is no variableness, neither shadow of turning."

Psalms 68:19 "Blessed be the Lord, who daily loadeth us with benefits,

even the God of our salvation. Selah."

When we were saved, and then born again of the Holy Spirit, God wiped out all of our past. He wiped out our old identity - every single thing the devil had over us. Christ Jesus totally wiped it out, and nailed it to the Cross. God changes us from the inside out, and His Holy Spirit anoints us for battle - in Christ. Our life is now a life of faith. This is how we are to live. By faith.

Galatians 2:20 **"I am crucified with Christ: nevertheless I live; yet not I, but Christ liveth in me: and the life which I now live in the flesh I live by the faith of the Son of God, Who loved me, and gave himself for me."**

Philippians 2:13 **"For it is God which worketh in you both to will and to do of his good pleasure."**

It is essential that every Christian know their identity in Christ, because the devil will take advantage of those who don't know their identity. Start confessing what God's Word says about your identity in Christ. Don't let some man tell you. Don't let the devil whisper in your ear. Get into the Word of God and stand upon all the promises. Proclaim who you are in Christ. The seven sons of Sceva tried to use the Name of the Lord Jesus to cast out evil spirits - without even having a relationship with Him. The only way a person can have authority to use His Name and cast out demons is to be IN CHRIST. The seven sons of Sceva tried to no avail - because the evil spirits did not recognize them.

Acts 19:13-16 **"Then certain of the vagabond Jews, exorcists, took upon them to call over them which had evil spirits the name of the Lord Jesus, saying, We adjure you by Jesus whom Paul preacheth. And**

there were seven sons of one Sceva, a Jew, and chief of the priests, which did so. And the evil spirit answered and said, Jesus I know, and Paul I know; but who are ye? And the man in whom the evil spirit was leaped on them, and overcame them, and prevailed against them, so that they fled out of that house naked and wounded."

They recognized Jesus of course, and they recognized Paul, but not these so called exorcists. It just shows the advantages to being in Christ, and the disadvantages to not being in Christ. If we truly want to be anointed for battle, and overcome all things, then we had better know who we are in Christ, as well as our authority in Christ. Another part of our identity in Christ is knowing that we are the body of Christ. Jesus is the Head, and we the anointed Church, are His body. When we are baptized in the Holy Spirit - He adopts us into His body.

Galatians 3:27 "For as many of you as have been baptized into Christ have put on Christ."

Romans 8:15 "For ye have not received the spirit of bondage again to fear; but ye have received the Spirit of Adoption, whereby we cry, Abba, Father."

1 Corinthians 12:13-14 "For by one Spirit are we all baptized into one body, whether we be Jews or Gentiles, whether we be bond or free; and have been all made to drink into one Spirit. For the body is not one member, but many."

There are many Scriptures that clearly show us that we are the body of Christ. Let's look at a few of them.

1 Corinthians 12:27 "Now ye are the body of Christ, and members in particular."

Colossians 1:18 **"And he is the head of the body, the church: who is the beginning, the firstborn from the dead; that in all things he might have the preeminence."**

Romans 12:5 **"So we, being many, are one body in Christ, and every one members one of another."**

Ephesians 1:22-23 **"And hath put all things under his feet, and gave him to be the head over all things to the church, which is his body, the fullness of him that filleth all in all."**

We see right there in the Word of God that we, the Church, are the body of Christ. There are no doubts about it. Now that we know that we are the body of Christ, then who is the bride of Christ? Well, through a lot of traditional teaching, there have been many people teaching that the Church is the bride, however, this is not confirmed by Scripture. The Church is not the bride of Christ. In fact, there is not one single verse in the Bible that says the Church is the bride. The misconception most likely comes from the misusing of certain Scriptures in the Bible. One of the most used is Ephesians chapter 5 verses 22-33. However, if you clearly study the context of these verses, you will see that Christ is only giving a comparison of the husband and wife relationship to the relationship between Christ and His Church. Let's look at verses 22-25:

Ephesians 5:22-25 **"Wives, submit yourselves unto your own husbands, as unto the Lord. For the husband is the head of the wife, even as Christ is the head of the church: and he is the savior of the body. Therefore as the church is subject unto Christ, so let the wives be to their own husbands in everything. Husbands, love your wives, even as Christ also loved the church, and gave himself**

for it."

Notice verse 23, it says Christ is the Savior of the body. It doesn't say He is the Savior of His bride. Just because it is talking about husbands and wives in these passages, does not mean that the Church is the bride. We are clearly His body, and the body only. Just think about it this way - if we were the bride, then we could not have intimacy until after the wedding, because if we did, we would be committing fornication, which is clearly a sin. However, we have intimacy with Christ now because we are His body, not His bride. Christians who think they are the bride are really deceiving themselves. Just because many people believe something to be true, doesn't mean that it is. As in every doctrine, we must have a firm Scriptural foundation on which to stand. The Bible says that we, the Church, are the body of Christ. That is our identity. Not as the bride. Now that we know our identity in

Christ as His body, we need to find out who the bride is. Let's read in Revelation chapter 21:

Revelation 21:2, 9-10 **"And I, John saw the holy city, new Jerusalem, coming down from God out of heaven, prepared as a bride adorned for her husband."**

Verses 9-10 **"And there came unto me one of the seven angels which had the seven vials full of the seven last plagues, and talked with me, saying, Come hither, I will shew thee the bride, the Lamb's wife. And he carried me away in the Spirit to a great and high mountain, and shewed me that great city, the holy Jerusalem, descending out of heaven from God."**

So we see right here in Revelation chapter 21, that the identity of the bride of Christ is the city of New Jerusalem. In the Old Testament, the future marriage of the city of Jerusalem was proclaimed:

Isaiah 62:1-5 "For Zion's sake will I not hold my peace, and for Jerusalem's sake I will not rest, until the righteousness thereof go forth as brightness, and the salvation thereof as a lamp that burneth. And the Gentiles shall see thy righteousness, and all kings thy glory: and thou shalt be called by a new name, which the mouth of the Lord shall name. Thou shalt also be a crown of glory in the hand of the Lord, and a royal diadem in the hand of thy God. Thou shalt no more be termed Forsaken; neither shall thy land any more be termed Desolate: but thou shalt be called Hephzibah, and thy land Beulah: for the Lord delighted in thee, and thy land shall be married. For as a young man marrieth a virgin, so shall thy sons marry thee: and as the bridegroom rejoiceth over the bride, so shall thy

God rejoice over thee."

We, the body of Christ, with Jesus at our Head, will be married to New Jerusalem - which is the bride. At the marriage Supper of the Lamb, the bride - the New Jerusalem, makes herself ready for the wedding. The wedding gown is decorated with our righteousness - the righteousness we have been made in Christ. We are in Christ, and Christ is in us, so therefore not only does Jesus have a bride, but so do we because we are one with Him as His body. We are a part of the bridegroom.

Revelation 19:7-8 **"Let us be glad and rejoice, and give honour to him: for the marriage of the Lamb is come, and his wife hath made herself ready. And to her, was granted that she should be arrayed in fine linen, clean and white: for the fine linen is the righteousness of saints."**

In many places in Scripture, mostly in Revelation, we see that Jesus tells the Church - His body, to have ears to hear what the Holy Spirit says. We, the anointed body of Christ, as part of the bridegroom - are also called His friends. His friends hear His voice, and rejoice in Him.

Revelation 3:22 **"He that hath an ear, let him hear what the Spirit saith unto the churches."**

John 3:29 **"He that hath the bride is the bridegroom: but the friend of the bridegroom, which standeth and heareth him, rejoiceth greatly because of the bridegroom's voice: this my joy therefore is fulfilled."**

In Revelation 22 we see that the Holy Spirit and the bride - New Jerusalem, are giving a call to all those who have ears to hear.

Revelation 22:17 **"And the Spirit and**

the bride say, Come. And let him that heareth say, Come. And let him that is a thirst come. And whosoever will, let him take the water of life freely."

It's time for the true Church to take a stand and proclaim their identity and birthright in Christ. Don't forfeit your birthright and inheritance by embracing traditions of men, and idolatry. Doing so could cause you to lose your place in the eternal body of Christ. The Word says to flee from idolatry:

1 Corinthians 10:14 "Wherefore, my dearly beloved, flee from idolatry."

Hebrews 12:14-17 "Follow peace with all men, and holiness, without which no man shall see the Lord: Looking diligently lest any man fail of the grace of God; lest any root of bitterness springing up trouble you, and thereby many be defiled: Lest

there be any fornicator, or profane person, as Esau, who for one morsel of meat sold his birthright. For ye know how that afterward, when he would have inherited the blessing, he was rejected: for he found no place of repentance, though he sought it carefully with tears."

One more thing I would like to add, and you really need to think about this. If the Church were the bride, then that would mean that Jesus would be marrying Himself. How absurd that would be, right? So obviously, we are the body, and not the bride. God is calling His people to a deeper place, a higher place in Him, It's not enough just to barely get saved, then go about life never growing in the things of God. The Lord has so much more for us, and we need to come up higher in Him, and be sensitive to the leadings of His Spirit. Now, more than ever before, God's people need to get into that deeper place in their walk with

Him.

THE DEEPER THINGS OF GOD:

Psalms 42:7 **"Deep calleth unto deep at the noise of thy waterspouts, all thy waves and thy billows are gone over me."**

The deeper things of God are all available to us - right in His presence, and through the power of the Holy Spirit. Believers must have a love for all of God's Truth, and a love for Him that outweighs any love we have in the natural realm. God and His kingdom must be first place in our lives.

Matthew 6:33 **"But seek ye first the kingdom of God, and his righteousness; and all these things shall be added unto you."**

Far too often, Christians get so caught up in other things, that they lose sight of the greater things that God has for them. To walk as an anointed warrior ready for battle, we must be completely obedient unto God, and have ears to hear what the Holy Spirit is speaking to us. In the book of Luke, we see two sisters, Mary and Martha of Bethany. Mary sat at the feet of Jesus and heard His Word. She was a worshipper, and she had her priorities straight. Her sister Martha was another story. She was a worry wart, who was always busy, busy. She had her priorities all messed up. Jesus gave her a rebuke, and told her that her sister Mary has chosen what is good, and that it will not be taken from her. She chose to establish the priority of putting God and His kingdom first.

Luke 10:38-42 **"Now it came to pass, as they went, that he entered into a certain village: and a certain woman named Martha received him into her house. And she had a sister called Mary, which also sat at Jesus feet, and heard His word. But Martha**

was cumbered about much serving, and came to him, and said, Lord, dost thou not care that my sister hath left me to serve alone? Bid her therefore that she help me. And Jesus answered and said unto her, Martha, Martha, thou art careful and troubled about many things: But one thing is needful: and Mary hath chosen that good part, which shall not be taken away from her."

Isn't that how it always is? Someone is truly following God and worshipping Him, and someone else comes along and gets mad and jealous. The thing is, we all need to learn to sit at the feet of Jesus, and learn to listen to His Word. We need to worship Him in Spirit and in truth, and put Him first place in our lives. When we do, we will move into the deeper things, into the higher realm. God is looking for the true worshippers!

John 4:23-24 **"But the hour cometh,**

and now is, when the true worshippers shall worship the Father in spirit and in truth: for the Father seeketh such to worship him. God is a Spirit: and they that worship him must worship him in spirit and in truth."

Psalms 95:6-7 a "O come , let us worship and bow down: let us kneel before the Lord our maker. For he is our God; and we are the people of his pasture, and the sheep of his hand"

The more we thirst after God's presence, the greater the anointing will come upon us and empower us. We will be saturated in God's manifest presence, and others will want to have what we have. That hunger for more of Him needs to be greater than anything else in our lives.

Psalms 42:1-2 "As the deer pants for the water brooks, so pants my soul for You, O God. My soul thirsts for God, for the living God. When shall I come and appear before God?"

(NKJV)

When we receive the Holy Spirit, we are given the revelations and mysteries of God and His kingdom. God reveals His deeper things by the Holy Spirit Who dwells in us - when we are baptized in the Holy Spirit. We cannot look to man's wisdom, because man's wisdom is limited. We have to look to and rely on the Holy Spirit, for He is our Teacher, and He will reveal deep things - even mysteries that the natural man can't comprehend. Let's read now in first Corinthians chapter 2:

1 Corinthians 2:4-5, 9-16 **"And my speech and my preaching was not with enticing words of man's wisdom, but in demonstration of the Spirit and of power: That your faith should not stand in the wisdom of** men, but in the power of God."

Verses 9-16 "But as it is written, eye hath not seen, nor ear heard, neither have entered into the heart of man, the things which God hath prepared for them that love Him. But God hath revealed them unto us by His Spirit: for the Spirit searcheth all things, yea, the deep things of God. For what man knoweth the things of a man, save the spirit of man which is in him? Even so the things of God knoweth no man, but the Spirit of God. Now we have received, not the spirit of the world, but the Spirit, which is of God; that we might know the things that are freely given to us of God. Which things also we speak, not in the words which man's wisdom teacheth, but which the Holy Ghost teacheth; comparing spiritual things with spiritual. But the natural man receiveth not the things of the Spirit of God: for they are foolishness unto him: neither can

he know them, because they are spiritually discerned. But he that is spiritual, judgeth all things, yet he himself is judged of no man. For who hath known the mind of the Lord, that he may instruct him? But we have the mind of Christ."

We have the mind of Christ, so the deep things of God are readily available to us. Our job is to believe and seek God, and let the anointing of the Holy Spirit saturate every fiber of our being. The anointing will not flow unless we are in true fellowship with God and with His people. The anointing flows when there is unity, but when unity and full agreement is not present, the Holy Spirit is grieved, and His power is quenched. That's not a place to be. The Scriptures clearly show this.

1 Thessalonians 5:19 **"Quench not the Spirit."**

Ephesians 4:30 "And grieve not the Holy Spirit of God, whereby ye are sealed unto the day of redemption."

Psalms 133:1-3 "Behold, how good and how pleasant it is for brethren to dwell together in unity! It is like the precious ointment upon the head, that ran down upon the beard, even Aaron's beard: that went down to the skirts of his garments; As the dew of Hermon, and as the dew that descended upon the mountains of Zion: for there the Lord commanded the blessing, even life for evermore."

God's commanded blessings will come in the place where the anointing of the Holy Spirit is present, and where there is unity with God and with true believers. This in unity in the Spirit, and will bring a fresh anointing upon us, making it easier to flow in the deeper things of God. On the Day of Pentecost, the people came together in one accord - in unity, and were baptized in the Holy Spirit with the evidence of tongues.

Acts 2:1-4 **"And when the day of Pentecost was fully come, they were all with one accord in one place. And suddenly, there came a sound from heaven as of a rushing mighty wind, and it filled all the house where they were sitting. And there appeared unto them cloven tongues like as of fire, and it sat upon each of them. And they were all filled with the Holy Ghost, and began to speak with other tongues, as the Spirit gave them utterance."**

The anointed power of the Holy Spirit came upon all of them, and instantly they were translated into a higher and deeper realm in God. They were anointed for battle. This was the true beginning of the anointed Church. This is when believers really started to move in the deeper things of God. This is how we are truly empowered for evangelism. The anointing of the Holy Spirit upon us and in us is present to destroy every yoke of bondage, and will remove every burden off of every shoulder.

***Isaiah 10:27* "And it shall come to pass in that day, that his burden shall be taken away from off thy shoulder, and his yoke from off thy neck, and the yoke shall be destroyed because of the anointing."**

As we go from glory to glory, the anointing upon us becomes stronger, because the latter house is greater than the former house (temple). We are being changed into the image of Christ Jesus our wonderful Lord and Savior.

***2 Corinthians 3:17-18* "Now the Lord is that Spirit: and where the Spirit of the Lord is, there is liberty. But we all, with open face beholding as in a glass the glory of the Lord,**

are changed into the same image from glory to glory, even as by the Spirit of the Lord."

Haggai 2:1-9 "In the seventh month, in the one and twentieth day of the month, came the word of the Lord by the prophet Haggai, saying, Speak now to Zerubbabel, the son of Shealtiel, governor of Judah, and to Joshua the son of Josedech, the high priest, and to the residue of the people, saying, who is left among you that saw this house in her first glory? And how do ye see it now? Is it not in your eyes in comparison of it as nothing? Yet now be strong, O Zerubbabel, saith the Lord; and be strong, O Joshua, son of Josedech, the high priest; and be strong, all ye people of the land; saith the Lord, and work: for I am with you, saith the Lord of hosts: According to the word that I covenanted with you when ye came out of Egypt, so my Spirit remaineth among you: fear ye

not, for thus saith the Lord of hosts; Yet once, it is a little while, and I will shake the heavens, and the earth, and the sea, and the dry land; And I will shake all nations, and the desire of all nations shall come: and I will fill this house with glory, saith the Lord of hosts. The silver is mine, and the gold is mine, saith the Lord of hosts. The glory of this latter house shall be greater than of the former, saith the Lord of hosts: and in this place will I give peace, saith the Lord of hosts."

We, the body of Christ, are the latter house - the latter temple. God spoke to the Old Testament prophets about events that would be relevant for the latter generation. Some of it applied to their time, but a lot of it is talking about end-time events for the last generation, which is us - the body of Christ, the true anointed Church. God gave Haggai the prophecy of the final shaking of all things, and that the glory of the body of Christ - the latter temple, would be revealed. There's definitely going to be a final shaking of all people, and the final result will be the glorious, anointed latter temple (or house). In the New Covenant we have so much more than those who lived under the Old Covenant. The glory of the latter house will be greater than the former because we can be in the glory of God's kingdom, unspotted from the world and the devil's rotten agenda. We are more glorious because we have the Holy Spirit dwelling on the inside of us, anointing us for battle, anointing us to do even greater works than Jesus. We are the temple of the Holy Spirit, and as such - we need to be a beacon of light to this dark world.

***1 Corinthians 3:16-17* "Know ye not that ye are the temple of God, and that the Spirit of God dwelleth in you? If any man defile the temple of God, him shall God destroy; for the temple of God is holy, which temple**

ye are."

1 Corinthians 6:19-20 "What? Know ye not that your body is the temple of the Holy Ghost which is in you, which ye have of God, and ye are not your own? For ye are bought with a price: therefore glorify God in your body, and in your spirit, which are God's."

John 14:12 "Verily, verily, I say unto you, he that believeth on me, the works that I do shall he do also; and greater works than these shall he do; because I go unto my Father."

John 16:13-14 "Howbeit when He, the Spirit of truth, is come, He will guide you into all truth: for He shall not speak of himself; but whatsoever He shall hear, that shall He speak: and He will shew you things to come: He shall glorify me: for He shall receive of mine, and shall shew it unto you."

Far too many Christians focus on the natural, fleshly realm. We need to be focused on Christ, and the infusion we have with the Holy Spirit. Our eyes need to be opened to the deep revelations of the Spirit. The Church needs to hunger and thirst for more of God's presence. More of the depth and knowledge of His glorious Kingdom. The sad thing is, so much of the church has lost it's passion for God. A wake-up call is in order. The church needs to have their eyes of understanding enlightened with the revelation of God's Word. Let's read in Ephesians:

Ephesians 1:17-19 **"That the God of our Lord Jesus Christ, the Father of glory, may give unto you the Spirit of wisdom and revelation in the knowledge of him: the eyes of your understanding being enlightened; that ye may know what is the hope of his calling, and what the riches of**

the glory of his inheritance in the saints, and what is the exceeding greatness of his power to us-ward who believe, according to the working of his mighty power."

We need to ask the Lord to give us the Spirit of revelation and of His divine Wisdom. This will open our spiritual eyes to see more clearly into the deeper things of God. To all those who will believe - His power will be available to them. When we are rooted and grounded in Christ and in the Word, we will be able to comprehend all that pertains to God's kingdom. The very breadth, the length, the height, and the depth. Everything!

Ephesians 3:16-21 **"That he would grant you, according to the riches of his glory, to be strengthened with might by His Spirit in the inner man; That Christ may dwell in your hearts by faith; that ye, being rooted and grounded in love, may be able to**

comprehend with all saints what is the breadth, and length, and depth, and height; And to know the love of Christ, which passeth knowledge, that ye might be filled with all the fullness of God. Now unto him that is able to do exceeding abundantly above all that we ask or think, according to the power that worketh in us, unto Him be glory in the church by Christ Jesus throughout all ages, world without end. Amen."

The Holy Spirit is the Power that works in us, and with Him leading and guiding us, we are well on our way to glory. We need to also remember that the Holy Spirit has also provided spiritual Gifts for us to use, and they are all for today. Don't let anyone tell you any different.

1 Corinthians 12:8-11 **"For to one is given by the Spirit the word of wisdom; to another the word of knowledge by the same Spirit; to**

another faith by the same Spirit; to another the gifts of healing by the same Spirit; to another the working of miracles; to another prophecy; to another discerning of spirits; to another divers kinds of tongues; to another the interpretation of tongues: But all these worketh that one and selfsame Spirit, dividing to every man severally as He will."

These nine Gifts of the Holy Spirit are for the body of Christ, and God will divide these out to each member as He wills. Always be ready for God to use you in what ever way He chooses. It's mandatory that the body of Christ is on their guard, on the alert at all times. We cannot allow the deceit and trickery of the devil to hinder our calling in God. Remember, the devil can come very subtly, and use whomever he can to seduce you into his web of deceit. The devil can appear as light, and so can his followers. The devil is a master deceiver and an equal opportunity destroyer. Be watchful, and evict the devil and his lies out of your domain. There is only one Gospel, and that is the Gospel of Jesus Christ. Use discernment, and test everything - using the Word of God as your final authority. If it doesn't line up with the Word, then throw it out. It's that simple.

2 Corinthians 11:3-4, 13-15 **"But I fear, lest by any means, as the serpent beguiled Eve through his subtilty, so your minds should be corrupted from the simplicity that is in Christ. For if he that cometh preacheth another Jesus, whom we have not preached, or if ye receive another spirit, which ye have not received, or another gospel, which ye have not accepted, ye might well bear with him."**

Verses 13-15 **"For such are false apostles, deceitful workers, transforming themselves into the** apostles of Christ. And no marvel; for Satan himself is transformed into an angel of light. Therefore it is no great thing if his ministers also be transformed as the ministers of righteousness; whose end shall be according to their works."

Galatians 1:6-9 "I marvel that ye are so soon removed from him that called you into the grace of Christ unto another gospel: Which is not another; but there be some that trouble you, and would pervert the Gospel of Christ. But though we, or an angel from heaven, preach any other gospel unto you than that which we have preached unto you, let him be accursed. As we said before, so say I now again, If any man preach any other gospel unto you than that ye have received, let him be accursed."

The apostle Paul gives a very strict warning to all those who would pervert the true Gospel. A part of being anointed for battle, is recognizing the false, and casting it out. If it's not the Gospel of Jesus Christ, then it's another gospel, and needs to be rejected. Remember, we are to take up serpents, which includes casting out false doctrine.

Romans 16:17-18 **"Now I beseech you, brethren, mark them which cause divisions and offences contrary to the doctrine which ye have learned; and avoid them. For they that are such serve not our Lord Jesus Christ, but their own belly; and by good words and fair speeches deceive the hearts of the simple."**

Philippians 3:17-19 **"Brethren, be followers together of me, and mark them which walk so as ye have us for an ensample. (For many walk, of whom I have told you often, and now tell you even weeping, that they**

are the enemies of the cross of Christ: whose end is destruction, whose God is their belly, and whose glory is in their shame, who mind earthly things.)"

As the anointed Church, we are God's remnant. God's special people, and our conversation, our very citizenship is in heaven. This earth is just a dress rehearsal for heaven. We are training for reigning.

Philippians 3:20-21 "For our conversation is in heaven; from whence also we look for the Saviour, the Lord Jesus Christ"

1 Peter 2:9 "But ye are a chosen generation, a royal priesthood, an holy nation, a peculiar people; that ye should shew forth the praises of him who hath called you out of darkness into his marvelous light."

God's people have been called, and

appointed, and anointed for the battle. We are peculiar to those outside of the body, but that is a good thing - so was Jesus, and so were His disciples during His earthly ministry. Praise God, we are in very good company. Praise God we are a very peculiar people. God says we are His royal priesthood. You may say I don't look like royalty to you, but God says that I am, so it doesn't matter what you think. God's Word is my Source, and should be for every Christian. We are in the world, but not of it. There's a big difference, and we must understand it. Let's look at first John chapter 2:

***1 John 2:15-17* "Love not the world, neither the things that are in the world. If any man love the world, the love of the Father is not in him. For all that is in the world, the lust of the flesh, and the lust of the eyes, and the pride of life, is not of the Father, but is of the world. And the world passeth away, and the lust**

thereof: but he that doeth the will of God abideth for ever."

When we do the will of God, we will abide forever. The will of God is His Word. His will includes walking by faith, walking in obedience, and being an overcomer, and more than a conqueror. Being apathetic, lukewarm, wishy-washy, and complacent won't get it. We must be a Church without spot, wrinkle, or blemish. We must be a Church that is on fire for God, and we must allow His holy fire to empower righteousness and holiness, and burn up all the dross.

2 Corinthians 5:7 **"For we walk by faith, not by sight."**

Hebrews 10:38 **"Now the just shall live by faith: but if any man draw back, my soul shall have no pleasure in him."**

Hebrews 11:6 **"But without faith it is**

impossible to please him: for he that cometh to God must believe that he is and that he is a rewarder of them that diligently seek him."

The body of Christ is made up of faith people of a faith God. Apart from faith, we cannot please God. The Lord gives a very strong and straightforward statement to those who are lukewarm in the Letter to the Laodicean Church. Take heed to what He is saying:

Revelation 3:14-16 **"And unto the angel of the church of the Laodiceans write; These things saith the Amen, the faithful and true witness, the beginning of the creation of God; I know thy works, that thou art neither cold nor hot: I would thou wert cold or hot. So then because thou art lukewarm and neither cold nor hot, I will spue thee out of my mouth."**

In other words - if you are lukewarm

you make God sick. You're a bad taste in His mouth. At least those who are cold are not putting up a front. They know they're not serving God. Those that are lukewarm, however, think they are, but they are really just going through the motions. Lukewarm Christians have no desire to go to a higher, deeper level in God. They just want to stay where they are - in their comfort zone at ease. They are stale and stagnant, and a bad taste in God's mouth. Jesus goes on to tell the lukewarm Church to repent.

Revelation 3:19 **"As many as I love, I rebuke and chasten: be zealous therefore, and repent."**

Amos 6:1 **"Woe to them that are at ease in Zion, and trust in the mountain of Samaria, which are named chief of the nations, to whom the house of Israel came!"**

1 Corinthians 10:12 **"Wherefore let

him that thinketh he standeth take heed lest he fall."

There's no time for playing games with God. It doesn't work. God is a holy God, and He wants our undivided attention. He wants a Church that is obsessed with Him. We need to be a Church on fire, whose flame burns up all that opposes God's holy kingdom. The very fire of Almighty God!

Psalms 97:3 **"A fire goeth before him, and burneth up his enemies round about."**

We, the Church that have been anointed and equipped for battle, have an inheritance awaiting us. A full inheritance. It is eternal, and is available to all those who will overcome, and follow Christ Jesus no matter what. The inheritance starts now, and will be completed once we are glorified and raptured.

Revelation 3:21 "To him that overcometh will I grant to sit with me in my throne, even as I also overcame and am set down with my Father in his throne."

Colossians 1:12 "Giving thanks unto the Father, which hath made us meet to be partakers of the inheritance of the saints in light."

THE PRE-TRIBULATION RAPTURE:

As I mentioned earlier in this book, the next big event on God Almighty's time-table is the Pre-tribulation Rapture of His Church, the body of Christ. This anointing for battle I have been talking about is leading us up to this joyful event. When we truly know how to use our spiritual weapons and our authority, we will demolish the devil's agenda, and be in place for glory. When we truly know who we are in Christ, and know our rights and privileges as a King's kid, the devil will be putty in our hands. Remember, the anointing is not to be taken lightly - it is the very presence of God the Holy Spirit that destroys yokes, removes burdens, and pulls down strongholds. We cannot allow the devil to trip us up through his wiles, or through false doctrine. We must embrace the Truth, which is God's Word, and march forth as the anointed Army of God who will soon be glorified, and caught up to meet the Lord Jesus in the air. There's absolutely nothing on this earth that is worth losing our full inheritance. Very soon, in the twinkling of an eye, we are going to be glorified! Like I said, the Rapture of the church is BEFORE the tribulation. We, the anointed church, are the restraining force that holds back the Antichrist. Once we are removed from this earth, via the Rapture, then the Antichrist will rise on the scene and set up his one world order.

2 Thessalonians 2:6-8 "**And now you know what is restraining, that he may be revealed in his own time. For the mystery of lawlessness is already at work: only He who now restrains will do so until He is taken out of the way.**"
(NKJV)

After we are taken up to heaven, all chaos will take place upon the earth. The tribulation will be a time like nothing ever before. You don't want to be a part of it. You need to choose today to be a part of the true church which will be glorified in the twinkling of an eye. Let's look at first Corinthians 15, followed by a few other Scripture passages:

1 Corinthians 15:50-58 "**Now this I say, brethren, that flesh and blood cannot inherit the kingdom of God; neither doth corruption inherit incorruption. Behold, I shew you a** mystery; We shall not all sleep, but we shall all be changed, In a moment, in the twinkling of an eye, at the last trump: for the trumpet shall sound, and the dead shall be raised incorruptible, and we shall be changed. For this corruptible must put on incorruption, and this mortal must put on immortality. So when this corruptible shall have put on incorruption, and this mortal shall have put on immortality, then shall be brought to pass the saying that is written, Death is swallowed up in victory. O death, where is thy sting? O grave, where is thy victory? The sting of death is sin; and the strength of sin is the law. But thanks be to God, which giveth us the victory through our Lord Jesus Christ. Therefore, my beloved brethren, be ye steadfast, unmovable, always abounding in the work of the Lord, forasmuch as ye know that your labour is not in vain in the Lord."

Hebrews 9:28 "So Christ was once offered to bear the sins of many; And unto them that look for him shall he appear the second time without sin unto salvation."

1 John 3:2 "Beloved, now are we the sons of God, and it doth not yet appear what we shall be: but we know that when he shall appear, we shall be like him; for we shall see him as he is."

Colossians 3:4 "When Christ, who is our life, shall appear, then shall ye also appear with him in glory."

The true body of Christ is going to be glorified and changed from corruption to incorruption, glory be to God. Our fleshly bodies are going to be made and fashioned like unto His glorious body.

Philippians 3:20-21 "For our

conversation is in heaven; from whence also we look for the Saviour, the Lord Jesus Christ: Who shall change our vile body, that it may be fashioned like unto his glorious body, according to the working whereby he is able even to subdue all things unto himself."

We see the actual Rapture of the Church in 1 Thessalonians chapter 4, when we will be literally transported to heaven to live for all eternity. What a glorious event this will be! Are you rapture ready?

1 Thessalonians 4:16-18 **"For the Lord himself shall descend from heaven with a shout, with the voice of the archangel, and with the trump of God: and the dead in Christ shall rise first: Then we which are alive and remain shall be caught up together with them in the clouds, to meet the Lord in the air: and so shall we ever be with the Lord.**

Wherefore comfort one another with these words."

Titus 2:13-14 "Looking for that blessed hope, and the glorious appearing of the great God and our Savior Jesus Christ; Who gave himself for us, that he might redeem us from all iniquity, and purify unto himself a peculiar people, zealous of good works."

Daniel 12:1-3 "And at that time shall Michael stand up, the great prince which standeth for the children of thy people: and there shall be a time of trouble, such as never was since there was a nation even to that same time: and at that time thy people shall be delivered, every one that shall be found written in the book. And many of them that sleep in the dust of the earth shall awake, some to everlasting life, and some to shame and everlasting contempt. And they that be wise shall shine as

the brightness of the firmament; and they that turn many to righteousness as the stars for ever and ever."

Don't be foolish and let your lamp go out. Be wise and keep your lamp burning with the oil of the Holy Spirit. The unwise, lukewarm will be left behind, but those who are full of oil, and awaiting the Savior - will be caught up to be with Him, and to be sitting with Him on His holy throne. Let's take a look at the Parable of the ten virgins. Five of them were wise, and five of them were foolish. This parable is a type for the Rapture of the Church:

Matthew 25:1-13 **"Then shall the kingdom of heaven be likened unto ten virgins, which took their lamps, and went forth to meet the bridegroom. And five of them were wise, and five were foolish. They that were foolish took their lamps, and took no oil with them: But the** wise took oil in their vessels with their lamps. While the bridegroom tarried, they all slumbered and slept. And at midnight there was a cry made, Behold, the bridegroom cometh; go ye out to meet him. Then all those virgins arose, and trimmed their lamps. And the foolish said unto the wise, Give us of your oil; for our lamps are gone out. But the wise answered, saying, Not so; lest there be not enough for us and you: but go ye rather to them that sell, and buy for yourselves. And while they went to buy, the bridegroom came; and they that were ready went in with him to the marriage: and the door was shut. Afterwards came also the other virgins, saying, Lord, Lord, open to us. But he answered and said, Verily I say unto you, I know you not. Watch therefore, for ye know neither the day nor the hour wherein the Son of man cometh."

Proverbs 3:35 "The wise shall inherit glory: but shame shall be the promotion of fools."

Matthew 7:21-27 "Not every one that saith unto me, Lord, Lord, shall enter into the kingdom of heaven; but he that doeth the will of my Father which is in heaven. Many will say to me in that day, Lord, Lord, have we not prophesied in thy name? and in thy name have cast out devils? And in thy name done many wonderful works? And then will I profess unto them, I never knew you: depart from me, ye that work iniquity. Therefore, whosoever heareth these sayings of mine, and doeth them, I will liken him unto a wise man, which built his house upon a rock: And the rain descended, and the floods came, and the winds blew, and beat upon that house; and it fell not: for it was founded upon a rock. And every one that heareth these sayings of mine,

and doeth them not, shall be likened unto a foolish man, which built his house upon the sand: And the rain descended, and the floods came, and the winds blew, and beat upon that house; and it fell: and great was the fall of it."

There will be many whom Jesus will not know. Many will say Lord, Lord, open the door to us, and they will be shut out. They refused to walk in obedience to Christ. They refused the power and Gifts of the Holy Spirit. They refused to stop clinging to false doctrines. They went through the motions of being a believer, but didn't establish a true relationship with God. They may have done mighty works, but they were all done in vain. Their personal agendas got in the way. They refused to listen to the truth. Don't be one of those foolish, and disobedient sons who will be left behind for the tribulation. Choose today to be one of the wise who will inherit the eternal glory of God's kingdom. Choose to be a blood-bought, Spirit-filled, son of obedience, who knows who they are in Christ Jesus, who knows their spiritual weapons of warfare, who knows their God given authority, and who overcomes all things, and will hear those awesome words of our Lord Jesus - Come up hither. Choose today to be anointed for battle!

Luke 4:18-19 **"The Spirit of the Lord is upon Me, because He hath anointed me to preach the Gospel to the poor; He hath sent me to heal the brokenhearted, to preach deliverance to the captives, and recovering of sight to the blind, to set at liberty them that are bruised, to preach the acceptable year of the Lord."**

For more information about this ministry write to Pastor Shane Brown at:

The Prayer of Faith Ministry
P.O. Box 536
New Caney, Texas 77357

Call: 281-844-5216

E-mail:
prayerfaithministry@yahoo.com

Website:
www.prayerfaithministry.com